God, I Feel Like Cinderella!

My Supernatural Walk With God

W9-BDM-225

LuAnne Mast

Xulon PRESS

God, I Feel Like Cinderella!
My Supernatural Walk With God
by LuAnne Mast

Printed in the United States of America

ISBN 9781612157382

Portrait on front cover courtesy of Varano Photography.

Facebook LuAnne Mast
luannemast@gmail.com
eaglefireministries.com
www.destinydover.org
302-674-4288

www.xulonpress.com

Forewords

LuAnne Mast has blessed mankind with her testimony of God's supernatural power working in her life. Many saints will be encouraged and inspired to trust God's love and power to transform their lives. LuAnne's life testimony proves that God can take a life that has a dysfunctional childhood, an abusive marriage, and a seemingly helpless situation, and transform it into a life of joyful fulfillment.

The Lord Jesus promised to do exceedingly abundantly above all we could ask or imagine. Jesus said He came to bring us life and that more abundantly. You will see how God fulfills His Word in a person's life. Once you begin reading, you will not be able to lay this book aside until you have discovered all the supernatural and providential ways God worked in LuAnne's life.

Everyone needs to read this book for their own personal benefit. All who read this book will have faced similar situations as LuAnne, or will know someone that this book would help transform their life and give them a hope and a future.

Thanks, LuAnne, for sharing your life with so many people. You make me proud to be your Bishop. Many thousands shall be blessed by your testimony and supernatural ministry. God bless you and all who read your book.

Dr. Bill Hamon
Christianinternational.com
Two spaces after "Bishop" should be one. Justified alignment doesn't look right., Christian International Apostolic Network
Author: *Who Am I and Why Am I Here?, The Day of the Saints,* and many others.

This is a book that would bring great encouragement to anyone who has had the bottom fall out of their life. It's a great book depicting the emotional roller coaster of falling from prosperity to abject poverty to the total restoration of all things. The stories of God's supernatural intervention and His power, the working of the gifts of the Spirit and the miraculous divine appointments is not only encouraging but amazing. I found the book to be very interesting and edifying.

Randy Clark
Global Awakening Apostolic Network
Global School Of Supernatural Ministry
Author: *Changed in a Moment, Pressing In,* and many others.

"God I Feel Like Cinderella" is Powerful! Provoking! Penetrating! The scripture that comes to my heart is Psalm 126:1-2, "When the Lord brought back the captivity of Zion, we were like those who dream. Then our mouth was filled with laughter, and our tongue with singing. Then they said among the nations, "The Lord has done great things for them."" Glory is the goal in life. There is no greater purpose in life than to expose your personal glory by manifesting the Glory of God.

LuAnne's story is about a girl brought back to captivity; who has started to dream again. The testimony among the nations will be, "The Lord has done great things for her and He will do the same for me."

The book you are about to read starts like most good scripts, "Once upon a time…" What makes this story authentic is that every story has a villain. Even God's love story went from the beauty of a glorious beginning to betrayal and mutiny. As you finish this book it will end, "And they all lived happily ever after!", from pain to pleasure, nightmares to dreams, darkness to light, and guilt to glory, "Behold, I will make all things new" (Revelation 21:15).

Take your time to read this book and you will find God made you unique and irreplaceable. You will find out how incredibly precious you are, and the potential that has been buried inside of you will resurrect your life, "Call to me, and I will answer you, and show you great and mighty things, which you do not know" (Jeremiah 33:3). LuAnne has written a book that will make you want to worship and praise God. Take this journey towards greatness!

Leif Hetland
Author: *Seeing Through Heaven's Eyes, Healing the Orphan Spirit,* and many others.

This book is a journey of LuAnne's life! From abuse and dysfunction to a courageous woman of great faith. From lack and impossibilities to blessings and generosity. LuAnne represents Jesus Christ through releasing hope and a dependency on God's voice. I cried as I read between the lines of my friend's life, but I rejoiced as I saw how faithful God is. You will be encouraged as you read this book of LuAnne's childlike faith and God's supernatural power.
Sharon Stone
CIEurope.org

LuAnne Mast's story is both intriguing and wonderful. As you read her story there are many times that she could have easily crumpled into a heap and taken on a victim mentality. LuAnne's story takes away the excuses for anyone who believes that they should be able to give up because they are experiencing challenging times. In your hands you hold a real-life Cinderella story.

When I first met her, I was doing a series of meetings in Utica, New York. My wife and I lost contact with her for over 10 years, but one day I was preaching in Texas and a familiar face walked up to me and said, "Do you remember me?" It took me a moment before I finally placed her. She was bold and confident. She had grown in stature and wisdom. She had grown in favor with God and man. "What!" I thought, "What happened to you over the last 10 years that brought you here? She had blossomed into a mighty woman of God with a powerful husband, pastoring a church together, and traveling the world. What a shock! The last I knew of LuAnne was that she was being challenged in every way, and now here she was standing with dignity and living a victorious life. I didn't really understand until I read the book that is in your hands. How could God take a victim and make her victorious? I was reminded of how much God watches over us as I read, "God, I Feel Like Cinderella." Receive strength and hope as you see God's delivering hand in LuAnne's story.

Pastor Tracey Armstrong
citadelchurch.com
LionHeartMinistries.com
Author: *Followership, Becoming a Pioneer of Success*

I have had the joy of watching the Lord restore the things that had been stolen from LuAnne's life. I have marveled at the Lord's healing and even recreating the parts of LuAnne's life that were broken beyond recognition. Her story is a Cinderella story in the way she came from a humble and abusive background to marry her prince and rule over the enemies who opposed her. Like a modern-day Cinderella story, God's grace beat all odds stacked against LuAnne to give her victory. I know that many reading her story will relate to the hopelessness she felt early in her life. LuAnne's story is the story of God's ability to reach into a broken life, pick up the pieces, and create a beautiful showpiece with it. When most people would see broken glass as only good for the rubbish heap, the skilled artist forms a beautiful mosaic. Our Savior took the broken pieces of LuAnne's life and formed an image of His grace for all the world to marvel at. May LuAnne's story give each reader hope and the ability to see the hand of God in their life. Like a real-life Cinderella, He makes beauty from ashes.

Lon R. Dean
Lead Pastor
House of Praise
www.houseofpraise.cc/

I was moved to tears as I read LuAnne's book. I first met her on a missions trip to Brazil in 2002. We have been close friends ever since. I personally watched her walk through many of the trials in this book. In spite all of these struggles, her faith in God and her love for Him never wavered. Scripture says that God is a rewarder of those who diligently seek him. LuAnne is now certainly reaping the rewards of her diligence. I would encourage everyone to read this book, as it reveals not only LuAnne's faith in God, but also God's faithfulness to her. What the enemy intended to destroy her with, God turned around and blessed her with. This is a true testimony of how through faith we can overcome even the most difficult circumstances.

Rick Sodmont
Humble Heart Ministries
Author: *The Father's Love*

I will always remember the first time I met LuAnne. I heard part of her testimony and watched her life of love being lived out right before my eyes. Little did I know that I was only hearing part of the story. What you are about to read is a real-life Cinderella story that will be difficult to put down. With each turn of the page, you will witness firsthand the goodness and grace of God extended to a woman who simply chose to say "Yes!" The book you hold in your hands is one woman's testimony, but it can also become a prophecy to be fulfilled in your own life. Happy reading!

Abner Suarez
Founder and President, For Such A Time As This, Inc.
Dunn, North Carolina

Life is not usually fair. Bad things happen to good people. Innocent lives are shattered by evil. Without God, mankind is controlled by his own unbridled instincts. Man, as his own god, is therefore capable of bringing pain, physical destruction, and mental torment to those in his path. Without God, these victims spend their lives in brokenness and hopelessness. But God!

God, Creator of the universe, has made it possible for hurting individuals to find a path of healing and restoration. In His great wisdom, God sent His Son, Jesus, to do more than offer eternal life to those who will accept His wonderful gift. He also made it possible for a person to be completely healed and given a fresh start in life. Broken, wounded people are able to experience a little heaven on earth. What a gift!

LuAnne Mast is a living testimony of the redeeming power of the Lord. Her vulnerability is evident throughout the book. She is open and honest as she relays her life stories filled with hurt and torment. However, LuAnne doesn't leave the reader filled with grief and remorse. She carefully weaves the story of redemption into her own story.

An important message from her book is this: *Your past is not your future!* There is hope for anyone walking through difficult days. Submitting your life totally to Jesus, learning the power of forgiveness, and standing firm in faith toward God positions a person to live an overcoming life.

LuAnne used her faith to propel her through the dark days of her past. She used that faith to move her forward into her future. Like Cinderella, LuAnne was willing to sweep away the ashes of her past. She found her prince and now enjoys the "happily ever after" life that only Jesus can bring.

You, too, may feel like Cinderella. Your life may be filled with ashes from past hurts, grief or shame. It is time to sweep away those ashes. Allow the Lord to awaken you to a new life. Let Prince Jesus carry you into your future. Your emotions will change. Like LuAnne Mast, you will find yourself shouting, "God, I feel like Cinderella!"

Barbara Wentroble
President – International Breakthrough Ministries
President – Breakthrough Business Network
President – Business Owners For Christ International
Author – *Fighting for Your Prophetic Promises, Removing the Veil of Deception, Prophetic Intercession, Praying With Authority*

Preface

Over the three years of our ministry together, I have seen firsthand the heart and ministry of LuAnne, my wife. God has given her a unique ability to connect to people's hearts and to be tremendously effective in breaking people free. I have seen many people open up areas of their lives to her that they never told anyone about. LuAnne's candid stories of her shortcomings, repentance, and faith in God create a safe environment for people to share their dark hidden pain, releasing healing. Shame has a way of silencing us with the threat of more rejection if we speak out. Yet talking about that shame is the beginning of healing. It is the beginning of accepting ourselves, separating our identity from abuse that occurred in our life, and turning it around towards God's purpose. I know this book will touch a part of your life in a unique way.

In Asia, one man came up to her for ministry after she shared her testimony of being abused. Laughing nervously he disclosed, "I abuse my wife." LuAnne looked at him for a moment and then asked a simple question: "Tell me, who abused you?" The man started weeping uncontrollably.

In another nation, we ministered over a weekend. The pastor's son, who had not attended church for over a year, would not even attend our meetings. He agreed to meet with

LuAnne and me privately after the last meeting. LuAnne ministered to him; his bitterness and unforgiveness were broken. His heart was released, and the lies he believed were removed. We saw him walking into the youth meeting smiling that very same day as we were leaving the church!

Women, from grandmothers to teenagers, confide in her after she shares her stories. For the first time in their lives, many confess to having had abortions or speak of abuses they have suffered. Men will share their stories as well. It really is quite amazing. I have been a senior pastor for almost thirty years, and I recognize that God has given LuAnne unique keys for unlocking people's deliverance.

There is a purpose for each story and the interaction of those involved. Each of us has been on different sides in different stories. Sometimes you were the angry person, sometimes you were the person receiving it. Every person needs healing from their life experiences.

The original purpose of this book was to help people see the supernatural power of God. If you need a great miracle, you have a great problem or great need. It takes a Goliath to reveal a David. Your most difficult challenges will mark who you are. It's never too late to try again.

LuAnne's life of faith and obedience will cause your faith "to run" again. Her stories will change your expectations, and will open your heart to dream and live again with God.

I will never forget how God brought LuAnne into my life. In addition to my deep love for her, God confirmed with sign after sign that He had brought her to be my wife. She is my princess and my Cinderella.

I love you, LuAnne.

Dale
destinydover.org
eaglefireministries.com

Contents

Chapter 7

Chapter 8

Chapter 9

Acknowledgments

I want to take the time to acknowledge those who are near and dear to me. They have helped me through my life's journey of making my life what it is today—blessed.

First and foremost, I thank you, Jesus, for restoring my broken life, removing the chains that bound me from abuse, shame, guilt, and condemnation. You gave me a hope and a future. You set me free! You're the best thing that ever happened to me.

To: Dale, the love of my life, my prince, my man of excellence, my encourager. Thanks for your love, support, prayers, and the happiest years of my life. Most of all, thanks for loving Mike and Matt. Thanks for pushing me to write this book and helping with it. I Love You!!!!! Oh yeah, thanks for the roses and the BMW☺

Mike and Matt, I love you and am so proud of you both. It was not easy for either of you. Mike, you gave me a lot of love and encouragement, and helped me to move on with my life. Matt, you were such a great support with your love, prayers and faith during some of my hardest challenges. You lived with me during the hard storms; sometimes it felt like we were drowning, but other times we walked on water! Thank you both for being there for me.

Ben, Heidi, Andrew and Zach, thanks for receiving me into your family. I love you guys.

Dad and Mom, I love you. I thank God that he gave me awesome parents. Dad, you always stood with me and for me. Mom, you always wanted the best for me. You both taught me the value of hard work, and how to manage a business.

To all my brothers and sisters, nieces and nephews, I love you and thank God for you. Brenda, thanks for washing my clothes and letting me use your shower.

Justin Stanislawski, thank you so much for all your hard work, wisdom, and endless hours editing my book as we kept adding stories.

Pastor Mike and Barb Servello, thank you for building the foundations of truth into my life that has been a great strength in my ministry. Thanks for all your love and prayers and support.

Pastor Lon and JoAnne Dean, thank you for teaching me never to give up, always believing in me, and teaching me how to set the captives free.

JoAnne Servello, thank you for your love, prayers and encouragement. You are an amazing woman of God. I love you. I miss Poppa.

Pastors at Mt. Zion—Mike Jr. and Mellissa, Charlie and Sharon Sweet, Chico and Lynn Woo, Rick and Clarissa Andrews, Steve and Marilyn Zuk, Dave and Leslie Nicollete, Paul and Patti Schilling, Mark and Stephanie Schilling, Sam and Sandra Luce, Charlie and Judy Piscillo—thank you for all your love, prayers and support, as well as the prophetic words that helped me go forward in the hard times.

Frank & Brenda Mellace, Thank you for your friendship, support and prayers, and all your time with my court battles and services you blessed my family with. Love you both.

Tina and Paul, Carleen, Freda, Bunnie, Mark and Kathy, Kelly Fleming, Pam and Paul Davis, Jim Cranford, Mike Clemente, Bill and Dianne Cook, Allahnisha, Erryl, Tom and Laura, Dan and Kathy, Cathleen and Billy, Mike and Cathy, Pat, Denise, Linda, Kelly Seminaro, Marilyn and Tony, Rhonda and Steve Lisi, Wanda and John, Mary and Rodger, Mel, Puffy, Carol, Barb and Dale, Justine, Christine, Norine, Shirley, Shada, Kim, Toni, Stephanie and Patrick, Pastors Ned and Sue, Pastors, Bill and Rita, Pastor Rose, Pastor Charity, Pastor Tony, Sophie, Cari Cash, Carol, Nita, Naim and Hakeem, Russell, Connie and Larry, Don and Pat Loguidice, Frank Thompson, Rick Sodmont and Debbie Isadore/Franco—I am so grateful for your friendship, prayer, love and support, and financial blessings for me and the boys. Love you all.

Peter Puleo, you taught me so much on the Holy Spirit and the glory. Thanks for being a great mentor and a great friend. I will never forget the last words that you spoke to me before you died: "LuAnne, promise me one thing: never give up on the supernatural." I never will.

Daughters of Zion, it was such a joy to minister and teach each of you over the years. Thanks for being there for me and all your prayers and support.

Norm and Suzi Audi—I miss you, Norm. I know you are enjoying heaven and you helped many to get there. You taught me much on deliverance and supported me financially many times. The very first time I met you in Brazil, you prophesied that my testimony would go all over the world. Suzi, you always demonstrated the love of God.

Pastor Tony, thanks for inviting me to be the assistant pastor with you at the Blessing Place. I will never forget the awesome things God did there.

The leaders at Destiny—Gary, Ashley, Jeff, Angie and Harry, and the family at Destiny Christian Church–it's a blessing having each one of you at Destiny. Thank you for your love and support and receiving me as your pastor.

Chapter 1

Escaping Death

It was a hot day after school, and I was ten years old and looking for some excitement. My friend Tammie and I were playing by the local lake. We dared each other to walk on the top of the dam to the other side of the lake. Before starting, we took off our shoes so they wouldn't get wet. I went first. It was fun feeling the force of the water with each step I took. The water was freezing!

As I approached the end of the dam there was a lot of green moss and the surface became very slippery. I slowed down and stepped very carefully. I was almost to the other side when my foot slipped. I fell from the top of the dam, smashing my head on the concrete as I fell into the water.

When my head hit, I thought I was going to die. I think I was semi-unconscious, yet I remember turning in the water. The water coming over the dam created an eddy that was spinning me around and forcing me to the bottom of the river. The water was very clear and I could see the stones at the bottom of the river. I felt so hopeless as the fear of death gripped me.

Then I felt a force pulling me up from the bottom against the current of the water and out from the churning river. The next thing I knew I was above the water, looking over at my friend. Then I worked my way to the bank of the river. She was standing at a distance from me. She was frantic! It all happened so fast.

There was no one there who could have pulled me out. I couldn't understand how I escaped. Now I know it was an angel or God's supernatural presence that saved my life. I find it difficult to explain exactly how it all happened. But one thing I know, I was miraculously saved from death! Tammie knew it too. Looking back now I realized why I was rescued: God had a purpose for my life that had not yet entered my thoughts as that daring little girl. I never expected to travel to the nations sharing my life stories. Nor could I grasp the impact my faith would have on so many people, as I shared the challenges that often felt insurmountable. It always releases peoples' faith to receive from God. So many people have said to me, "You should write a book. You have so many amazing stories!"

As the stories were gathered for this book, I could not believe all that I went through to get to my destiny. It was accomplished one miracle at a time. God is not distant or disconnected from our lives. May you see him as a God who loves, protects, and provides for you. I pray my story would build up your faith. As such, let's start from the beginning.

Growing Up In A Small Town

I grew up in a large family. I was one of nine children. There were six boys and three girls. I was the eighth child. My father worked for an oil company in addition to owning a bowling alley that he sold to buy a Tastee-Freez, an ice cream and fast food restaurant. My father, Jack, was a man of many talents. He actually built the beautiful house that we moved into on my first birthday. These words were written in the attic: "This is the house that Jack built."

My dad was a hard worker, and so was my mom. My siblings and I all started working from a young age, setting pins at the bowling alley or working at the Tastee-Freez. I started working at the Tastee-Freez at nine years old. My mom started us off by helping my dad cook in the back, but we would always sneak out front to wait on the customer window. That was the "grown-up" job, and making ice cream cones was the best part. It looked easy, but it actually took lots of practice.

My mother was going to stop having children after the first one. But her doctor told her a story about a woman who stopped having children after having four. They all died in a tragic fire. The woman lived the rest of her life without any children. The doctor would tell her this story every time she asked to have her fallopian tubes tied.

Well, the story worked, and my mom did not stop having children until the ninth one. If it hadn't been for that doctor, my mother would have never had me. I thank God for that doctor and his story. He actually delivered my first baby.

Growing up in a large family had its ups and downs. We shared the chores. We had our own baseball team! I shared my bedroom with two sisters. The three of us shared a regular-sized bed. As the youngest girl, I wore lots of "hand-me-downs." When I received my first paycheck, at nine years old, I bought new clothes. I refused to wear hand-me-downs anymore. I was involved in high school sports and activities. For family recreation, we went boating, snowmobiling, motorcycling, four-wheeling, and on many picnics. We never went on long-distance family vacations. I didn't leave that general area until I was nineteen. Visiting my Gram (grandmother) most weekends, shopping, team sports, and other activities took us to nearby towns, but that was it.

My childhood carried hidden pain and shame. I was sexually abused. My parents had no knowledge of it. I kept that secret hidden until I was thirty-seven.

My parents did not attend church. As a child, I asked my mom questions about God, and she told me as much as she knew. My sister Susie and I shared a bedroom after our sister Linda moved out. Susie and I used to lie awake at night and talk about God. She had such a love for God. She would watch Oral Roberts on TV and write him letters. I didn't know much about God, but I knew I loved Him. God was always very real to me. When I was ten years old, Susie took me to an Episcopal church that was just up the street. I joined the choir and was a teacher's aid in the classroom. Susie and I would walk home from church singing hymns. It brought a special joy. When I was sixteen, I attended the church's Bible studies and a prayer group to learn more about God. I had a real hunger for God.

It was the morning of July 4th, 1975, my friend Barb called to invite me to go out to a party with some friends who were going swimming. I said I would love to go. I was getting ready to leave when my mother told me I had to work a double shift at the Tastee-Freez because someone had called in sick. In the seven years of working there, I'd never had to work a double shift. I was very upset with my mother because it was my friend's party and I wanted to go.

Because of the July 4th holiday, the Tastee-Freez was exceptionally busy. Later that afternoon, Larry, a family friend, came up to the window to order a hamburger. He said, "Did you hear about Randy being killed? He was killed in an auto accident." Randy was a very popular athlete who had just graduated from high school. I was shocked to hear the news. He continued, "Barb was also killed in the accident. Steve is hurt and Debbie is in critical condition." I was devastated by the news! I would have been with them if I hadn't worked the double shift. Had I gone, I, too, could have been killed. It was very difficult for me to lose two close friends, and that tragedy impacted the entire town.

I never worked a double shift there again. It is even clearer to me now that God's supernatural intervention was in the natural events of that day. God used my mom and the sick employee to keep me from harm and even possibly death.

Who Did That?

On August 16, 1977, the day Elvis Presley died, I broke up with Tom, my long-time boyfriend. I felt I wasn't good enough for him. The shame in my life was controlling me. I started dating others. Between the ages of seventeen and eighteen, I had eight marriage proposals in eight months! I would start dating someone and they would propose to me. I would say "no" and end the relationship. I felt if they knew what had happened to me, they wouldn't want me. Because of the sexual abuse in my childhood, I never felt good enough for anyone.

After I broke up with Tom, I started going to bars. I took up drinking and staying out late. One night I was at the Rusty Nail, the bar I had been going to on weekends. I was talking to the bartender when a man walked behind me and pinched my butt. I turned around and told him, "You do that again and I will knock you on your ass!" The bartender said, "If you can knock him on his ass, I will give you seven shots of peach schnapps." Not more than two minutes later, he walked up to me and pinched me again. I turned around and punched that guy in the face. He flew back and fell to the floor, knocked out cold. The bouncers came over and asked, "Who did that?!" All the people around us pointed toward me and yelled, "She did!" They looked at me in unbelief and asked, "Did you really do this?" I was afraid of getting arrested, but I told them, "Yes, I did." They started laughing. I told them what he did to me. They picked him up off of the floor and threw him outside into a snow bank. I turned around and told the bartender, "Line them up!" I couldn't believe I was strong enough to do that. I knew it was anger inside that had been bottled up from my abuse.

On March 24, 1978, I went to the Rusty Nail; I met my soon-to-be husband for the first time. Let's say his name is "John Smith." We started dating the next week. Our relationship moved quickly, and we were engaged in less than three months. In August, we started building a house next to where his parents, grandparents, an uncle, and an aunt all had their homes. It was a modular Ridge Home. The shell of the house would be assembled, and then the owners would finish it. We worked on that house every night until we were married the following April. Many of his family were tradesmen, and they helped us with the plumbing, electrical contracting, cabinetry, flooring, and carpet installation.

My father and mother's engagement picture. They married Jan 1, 1947.

Me at 10 months old in front of the house my father built.

Me at 2 years old.

My brother Jeff and I
building a snow fort.

Me, my sister Susie and
Tammie at a birthday party.

I was in sixth grade, 9
years old.

Me and my niece, Brenda
at Thanksgiving 1971.

I was the Flaming
Foliage Queen my
Senior Year

My senior year book
picture

Me and my sister Susie at Easter.

My Graduation Day 1977.

I knocked the guy out in
the bar.

Chapter 2

More Pain And Shame

In September of 1978, I was frantic. I found out I was pregnant. I was so afraid to tell my mother. I knew how upset she would be. John and I had just built a house, and I didn't think that we could afford a baby. A few months passed, and I didn't tell anyone but him and my sister-in-law that I was pregnant. My sister-in-law told me where I could get an abortion. I made a wrong choice to have it. John drove me to the clinic in Buffalo, New York. The doctor called me into his office. He said, "Because of the potential for complications, I don't like to perform late-term abortions. I feel it's too late to proceed. But if you sign this waiver, I will go ahead with the procedure." I kept thinking about the guilt, the shame, and the condemnation of being pregnant. I didn't want to disappoint my mother. At the time, I thought having that abortion was the right decision. On the way home, it started to hit me. "Look what you've done! Why did you do that? You just killed your baby. You're an idiot!" It was terrible. I lived with that torment until the day I confessed the sin. Twenty years of torment. Every time I heard the word "abortion," my body would feel the pain of the loss I had experienced afterwards. Then the torment would start again.

A month before our wedding, John and I had a major argument. I gave him back my engagement ring as I was having second thoughts. We didn't talk for nearly two weeks. But, we had built a house together, and it had taken so much time and effort. The silent shame that I now carried from the abortion made me think, "You've made your bed, now sleep in it." So, I went back to him. When there is pain in your life, you think that something new will make you feel better and keep you moving forward. But pain you ignore just creates a path to more pain.

I was married in the local Catholic church at the age of nineteen. The night of the wedding rehearsal was a total disaster. My mom was smoking as she walked into the church. The priest yelled at her for entering the church with her lit cigarette. She walked over to a fixture on the wall she thought was an ashtray and put out her cigarette. She didn't know it was the Holy Water! At the back of the church, a loud argument broke out between my mom, my brother, and the priest. I thought the wedding was over.

The day of our wedding, the organist played the intro to the wedding march seven times. Each time, I couldn't move. My dad said, "What's wrong, LuLu?" I said, "I don't know, I can't move." I felt like something or someone was holding my legs from going forward. I was having second thoughts. But, I made the choice to go through with the marriage.

After the wedding, I kissed my mom goodbye. She said, "I love you." That was the first time I had ever heard her say that she loved me. The thought came to me, "You love me because I am out of the house." I realize now how the enemy talks to us. I believed his lie. I remember when I was younger, my friends would kiss their moms and dads goodbye and say, "I love you." I thought it was weird. One time I asked a friend, "Why do you say that? Isn't it weird?" After I was married, my mom would tell me that she loved me all the time. It was hard for me to believe it. It also made it difficult for me to receive love from other people.

Dale, who is now my husband (he enters the story later), has been a pastor for almost three decades. He has helped me understand this issue regarding my mom. She really did love me, but she was carrying her own pain. As I left the house, it was the tipping point that allowed her to say what she always felt. But I lived under the pain for many years of the unspoken love from my childhood.

First The Dog, Then Me

During our first week of marriage, John was working the midnight shift. I never wanted to be alone because of the abuse that had been in my life. So, we brought my mom's dog over to keep me company. Zebo, a toy poodle, had been our family's pet for many years. As soon as we got into our new house, Zebo peed on the kitchen floor. John went over, picked up Zebo, and threw him outside. Then he came back, picked me up, threw me outside, and locked the door behind me. He turned the porch light off and left me in the dark for an hour. That night I said to myself, "What the hell did I marry?"

Debbie, who was like a daughter to me, would stop by occasionally, even before I was married. Our families were close friends. After I was married, she would stay with me overnight when John worked the night shift. She was only nine years old when the following event happened: Debbie and I were in the living room. John came in and started yelling and shoving, and then hitting me. He was trying to take my car keys away. Debbie ran behind a chair to hide. She was afraid for me, but was also scared for herself. I threw her the car keys and told her to go to the car. I grabbed my purse and followed her out. We drove to my Mom's house. Later that day, I went home and John had calmed down. I never knew when he would explode with anger. It created a lot of fear in me.

Learning To Pray

During the first summer after I was married, a man selling books came to the house. He knocked on the back door, which was strange. When I opened the door, he forced himself inside the house. He started talking very loudly. I asked him to keep his voice down because my husband was sleeping. He asked, "Why would he be sleeping at this time of day?" I replied, "Because he works the midnight shift." This man kept demanding I buy his books. He said he needed the money "right now." I refused repeatedly, and he became very upset and left.

Around midnight, shortly after my husband left for work, I heard someone at the back door. They were turning the doorknob, trying to enter the house. I heard footsteps as they walked over the plywood that was temporarily covering the outside steps that led down into our basement.

All of a sudden it hit me–I had told this very disturbed young man that my husband was working the night shift. He must have been watching the house, waiting for John to leave. I grabbed Michael, my newborn son, and put him in the bed with me. I prayed frantically that this person would not be able to get into my home. Then I heard him trying to open the front door. I kept praying, and finally he gave up and left. Eventually I went to sleep. It turns out the police had issued a high-priority alert for this young man. They found him that next morning holding a young woman hostage with a knife at a trailer park. The situation ended after an extended standoff. My relationship with God was not that strong, yet my prayers were powerful before the Lord. He meets us where we are. He heard my cry.

That following summer, John kept trying to pick an argument with me. Then he walked into the bedroom and came out with his gun. He pointed it at me and threatened to kill me. I said, "Do what you have to do." He turned the gun around and threatened to kill himself. I ran out of the house to get John's father from next door. John's dad calmed him down. Eventually his dad drove the baby and me to my parents' house. My mom begged me not to go back. I didn't want my son to live without his father. He was really good with his son. He was also very good to me, except when his temper flared up.

During those years, I was managing the Tastee-Freez two nights a week. A teenaged girl named CeCe asked me if I was "saved." I said, "What does it mean to be saved?" She explained it to me. I told her I was Catholic. She said, "You will never forget it when it happens to you." Those words came back to me many years later. After seven years of living in the house we built, John took a job offer in North Carolina. It was a hard move because I had lived in that area my entire life.

The Blue Light Bandit

When I was twenty-eight, I was on my way home from the Raleigh-Durham airport when a car that had been following me turned on a blue flashing light. I couldn't see the car very well because its high beams were in my eyes. I pulled over to the side of the road, waiting for the policeman. As he walked from his car toward mine, I noticed he wasn't in uniform; nor was he wearing a hat. Something wasn't right, so I only rolled my window down about an inch.

When he came up to my window, he identified himself as a police officer. I thought it was weird he didn't ask me for my license or insurance card. He just wanted to know my name. Just then, my son Michael, who had been sleeping in the backseat, woke up and said, "Mommy, what's wrong?" I could tell this startled the "police officer." He abruptly stepped back and said, "I have another call." He ran back to his car and he took off.

I started shaking; something was very wrong. I was so thankful that he left. My son had woken up at just the right time. The next day I was reading the afternoon newspaper. It was reported that the police had just caught a man on the highway referred to as the "Blue Light Bandit." He was a rapist who prowled the interstate, looking for women who were alone.

From Loneliness To Deception

John and some of his coworkers had gone out of town for a "guys' weekend." That night I had taken my two sons to the movies. On the way home, my older son asked if we could stop by their school's football game to see who was winning. As we walked into the stadium, one of the coaches came up and started talking to me. Our conversation was brief. He asked me where their dad was, and I explained he was out of town on a business trip. It seemed like a very innocent conversion.

The phone rang after we returned home from the game. It was the coach whom I had just talked to. He asked I had made it home safely, because he knew I was alone. I thought it was so nice of him to check up on me, but it did seem a bit unusual. Nonetheless, it felt good that someone cared about me, and we talked for a while. I didn't realize how the enemy was setting me up for an affair.

That Sunday my husband returned home from his weekend of partying. He always acted weird and hateful to me after those party weekends. That night he started yelling at me and hitting me. Then he picked me up, threw me out the front door onto the concrete sidewalk, and locked me out of the house. He had done this to me many times in the other places we lived. This was not an unusual thing.

I had my car keys in my pocket, so I went for a drive. I stopped at a pay phone, called my coach friend, and told him what had just happened. He was at a pizza party with his children. He was a single dad, and his kids lived with him. He had a real heart for people, and was very concerned for me and how my husband was treating me.

Everyone thought John and I were the perfect couple. When he eventually left me, people were utterly shocked; they thought we were the model family. John was very involved with the boys in all of their sports activities. We went to mass together as a family every Sunday. He was very good to me in front of other people, and the boys never saw him hit me until the very last month of our twenty-three-year marriage.

John treated me well at times; on other occasions he was irritating and controlling. But when he got angry, it was unreal. He was abusive: verbally, mentally, and physically. Most of my shirts were torn at the neck from the abuse. After a night of hell, he would wake up as if nothing happened. He would buy me something nice after an "incident." I know it was sick, but sometimes I would almost look forward to the abuse to see what I would get out of it. He made me feel it was my fault. That is the nature of the spirit of abuse and the abuser. In many ways, I was codependent on him.

I felt as if I lived with two different people and had two lives. I didn't want to be divorced because I knew what it would do to my children. But I didn't want to be married to my husband either on account of his abusive patterns. In the beginning of the second year of our marriage, he started arguing with me about going to my mother's house as we were driving there. His anger exploded, and he slammed on the brakes and stopped the car. He told me to get out. I reached into the back seat and grabbed my four-month-old son; I walked for almost three miles before someone stopped to pick us up.

My coach friend seemed to care about me. I got a part-time job to make it easier to see him. I hated myself for living that way, so I quit my job. On my last night of work, I used my employee's discount for a neighbor who was making a layaway purchase. The total was just over $100. My boss called me into the office and asked me if I'd rung up that particular layaway. I said that I had. He said that the company was thinking about prosecuting me, and that they would notify me. I told him I was sorry. Two weeks later I received a phone call; the store manager said they were going ahead with the prosecution. He told me I needed to go to the police station to be booked. I couldn't believe they were prosecuting me for giving out that discount, but I know it was God getting my attention to deal with the affair.

When I walked into the police station, an officer asked me, "What's a nice lady like you doing in here?" I told him, "The store I worked for is prosecuting me for a discount I gave." The police officer laughed, asked me my name, and went to find the prosecution documents. The next thing I knew, I was getting fingerprinted and having my "mug shot" taken. It was very humiliating. There was a spirit of shame that came on me during that whole event. I had been a stay-at-home mom most of my marriage, and was afraid of what people would think of me.

As punishment, I ended up doing community service for a district attorney. He asked me to sit on the jury for a state supreme court case involving sexual abuse and the death of a child. The jury was split down the middle. The verdict came down to my decision. It was amazing that God allowed me to have a say over the spirit of abuse that I had battled with my whole life. After I finished the community service, I ended the affair. I couldn't handle the double life. I wanted to fix the mistakes I'd made, but didn't know how to do so. Soon afterward, my husband was transferred to another part of the state. I was so glad to move to away. I was running from the shame inside of me. Things were about to get worse, yet better.

Zebo, my mother's dog.

Debbie is the girl that I
threw my keys to as we ran
from the house.

Matthew and I

Michael and Matthew

Chapter 3

"Don't Touch That Dial"

It was the fall of 1992, and we had just moved across the state. I was thirty-three years old, and my sons were seven and twelve. It was a very difficult time in my life. My mother was diagnosed with cancer, and had just received a mastectomy. My sisters and I were advised to get tested for cancer. When I went, the doctor found a cyst the size of a grapefruit on my left ovary. The fear was overwhelming; it was paralyzing me. The guilt and the shame from my past made me feel like I deserved it. Because of the abuse in my past, always blaming myself seemed like a normal reaction. I thought God was punishing me for my sins. I was scheduled for surgery three weeks following.

During that time, my son Matthew woke up screaming and crying. He couldn't walk. I took him to the pediatrician. They thought my seven-year-old son had cancer in his leg and needed do more testing. Mike, our older son, was seeing an allergist. The apartment we moved into triggered his allergies from the previous renters' pets, and he was having a difficult time breathing. It seemed as if everything was crazy in my life. On top of that, we were struggling financially. We

hadn't yet sold our former house. We still had a house payment to make in addition to the rent on our apartment.

After taking the boys to school one morning, I returned
back to our apartment and sat down in the rocking chair,
emotionally drained. I turned on the TV and started flipping
through the channels. I heard a preacher say, "Are you sick
and tired of being sick and tired?" I thought, "He's talking
to me!" I was getting ready to change the channel when he
said, "Don't touch that dial!" I was shocked. It felt like he
was talking directly to me, so I continued to watch. He said,
"I know you know Jesus, but you don't know Him as your
Lord and Savior." I thought, "What does he mean by that?"
When I was eighteen, I had become a Catholic in order to
be married in the Catholic church. We went to mass every
Sunday as a family; we never missed a week. I didn't understand what he was talking about. Who was he to tell me that
I didn't know Jesus as my Lord and Savior?

The preacher, Robert Tilton, reiterated, "I know you
know Jesus, but you don't know Him as your Lord and
Savior. I want you to say this prayer with me and receive
Him in your heart. *'Jesus, come into my heart and be my
Lord and Savior. I ask You to forgive me of all my sins and fill
me with Your Holy Spirit.'"* I repeated the prayer and turned
off the TV. (If you have never asked Jesus to be your Lord
and Savior, you can repeat the prayer above. See Romans
10:13, "For *'whoever calls on the name of the LORD shall
be saved.'"*) That prayer changed my life forever.

I went upstairs to take a shower. As I was showering, a
huge ball of heat entered my body through my left ankle.
It went all the way up to the top of my leg, up through my
upper body, down my left arm, back up through my head,
down through my right arm and then it went all the way
down my right leg. I knew what had just happened to me was
something supernatural. I didn't understand it, but it felt like
a ball of heat.

Suddenly, I became very tired. I lay down and fell asleep for about two hours. It didn't make sense because I'd already had a good night's sleep and it was still morning. God was doing a deep work inside of me. He was beginning the healing process: healing pain from a life that had been filled with emotional, verbal, physical, and sexual abuse.

When I woke up, I knew the Lord had touched me deeply. I felt so refreshed and free. I knew something had changed dramatically in my life. I didn't understand it, but I knew I was different. Looking back, I see that my behavior started to improve rapidly. I used to swear frequently, but I stopped. Also, I found I didn't get angry like I used to. When I would get angry, it didn't affect me like it did before.

Then the miracles started! The cyst on my ovary was benign! It was removed three days before Christmas. My incision healed rapidly, and I was released from the hospital after a day. When I got home, I had so much energy that I started cleaning the house. The next day, my family and I decided to go to my parents' house for Christmas. It was an 11-hour drive. I surprised my mother for Christmas. She was amazed at how quickly God helped me recuperate from the surgery. She knew it was a miracle.

My son Michael's allergies settled down, and Matthew's doctor said an open bedroom window had caused a cold to settle in my son's hip, immobilizing it. Matthew was fine the next day!

When you are sick and tired of being sick and tired, it's a great time to look to God. What the enemy sent to destroy me, God used to draw me to Himself and display His awesome power. The healings and the answers to my prayers put a deep trust of faith and love of God in my heart. After accepting Jesus into my life, my first few days were so marked with the supernatural that it seemed normal for me to believe God for everything.

No Compromise

One morning my coach friend called. I immediately shared with him that I had become a Christian and had given my life to the Lord. I further shared that although I had grown up in church and thought I knew who Christ was, I had never received Him as my Lord and Savior. I asked my coach friend to forgive me for having an affair with him. Then I told him, "Please never call me again because I am going to make my marriage work." I finished by saying, "I pray that you would become a Christian." I hung up the phone and haven't talked to him since. I knew I had to take the initiative to end the relationship. After coming to the Lord, I realized that the affair was another type of abusive relationship. Affairs seem very comforting to those who have been abused, but they just end up piling on more pain and shame.

Coupon Miracles

I knew God had supernaturally done something in my life, so I started watching Robert Tilton every day on TV. When I would watch, I felt like God was talking to me. I remember Robert Tilton always spoke about making a vow unto the Lord. I didn't understand what a vow was, but I was obedient and vowed to give $100 to his ministry. I wasn't sure how I was going to pay it. I would send in any extra coupon money I had saved at the grocery store. It was often one or two dollars a week. I sent him my prayer requests, and it seemed as if God answered them all very quickly! I wrote back about all the miracles that God had done. His people called me and asked me to come on the show to talk about the miracles I'd received. I was surprised and blessed that they called me, but didn't want to be on television. My mom never liked cameras, and neither did I.

As soon as I made the first payment on that $100 vow, my husband received a promotion at work that included another immediate move from North Carolina to a plant in Pennsylvania. We were still making mortgage payments on a former house we'd lived in, as well as paying rent for the house in which we were at that time. But, I was trusting God for a financial miracle. Every day as I watched Robert Tilton's show, my faith increased.

About five months later, I took a letter with the last two dollars of the $100 vow to the mailbox. I paid this vow with the faith that God was going to help us sell our house in North Carolina. As I walked back into the house, the phone rang. It was my realtor from North Carolina. They had sold our house for cash, and he was sending me a check immediately! As soon as I hung up, the phone rang again. It was my husband telling me he was receiving a severance pay of $45,000 because of a title demotion from a previous job in North Carolina. I knew this happened as a result of the vow I had made to the Lord.

I shared this testimony with my parents. They were so excited for me. I could not stop praising God! We were now able to buy a home in Pennsylvania. I knew there was something supernatural about making a vow unto the Lord.

Miracles Exploding

I also ordered some prayer cloths from Robert Tilton. When I received them, I taped one over a large mole on my chest. When I woke up the next morning and pulled the prayer cloth off, the entire half-inch mole was inside it! It had fallen off! All of it was gone from my chest, and you couldn't even tell where it had been. Praise God! I was amazed by that miracle that God had done for me.

I also used a prayer cloth when my son Matthew, then seven years old, broke his arm. The day we moved into our new house in Pennsylvania, we decided to take a break from unpacking and go to the swimming pool. We went, and Matthew was playing on the nearby monkey bars. I had just finished putting on my suntan lotion, when Matthew came running around the corner with his arm hanging to his side. I could see the sadness and pain on his face as he yelled, "Mommy, I think I just broke my arm!" Not only had he broken his arm, but he had also dislocated his elbow. The emergency room doctor told us Matthew had broken his arm in two places and an orthopedic specialist was required for the surgery. The specialist put three pins in his elbow to hold it in place, and told Matthew that he would never again be able to use that arm to pitch. So we prayed and asked God to heal his arm, and slid a prayer cloth inside the cast. His doctor couldn't believe how quickly his arm and elbow healed! It wasn't long after that Matthew was pitching again! He was excellent in sports. He had a very strong arm in baseball, and often played third base or shortstop because of it.

My faith was growing to believe God for healing. I had hurt my back, and was in excruciating pain. Nothing I took or did relieved the pain. For three nights I slept in the recliner; it was a bit less painful than trying to lie flat." I watched Trinity Broadcasting Network (TBN) and the *700 Hundred Club* almost every day. It made such a difference in my spiritual growth. That day while watching Benny Hinn on TBN, he started praying for people who needed a healing. In the middle of his prayer I said, "God, with the faith that I have, I know that you can heal me." I felt the Lord say, "Stand up." At that moment, I stood up out of the recliner and was completely healed! The pain was gone! It was a miracle. For those first miracles, I'd used the prayer cloth as a focus for my faith. But for this one, God challenged me to physically move. So, I stood up as an act of faith. Faith requires action. We often call it a step of faith.

No More Soaps

"The lamp of the body is the eye. Therefore, when your eye is good, your whole body also is full of light. But when *your eye* is bad, your body also *is* full of darkness. Therefore take heed that the light which is in you is not darkness. If then your whole body *is* full of light, having no part dark, *the* whole *body* will be full of light, as when the bright shining of a lamp gives you light" (Luke 11:34–36).

Before I was saved, I used to watch soap operas every day. I was addicted! I never missed *Guiding Light* or *Knot's Landing*. After accepting Christ, I started watching Christian TV as well. Three months later the Holy Spirit spoke to me and told me not watch the "soaps" anymore. So, I obeyed. This was another miracle because I was really hooked on those stories. My life used to be wrapped up in those stories, but now my life was in Jesus. Christian TV was all I had time for. Many people cannot enter into what God has for them, because they are not willing to give up the things that displease Him. What fills your eyes and ears will fill your heart. What is in your heart will become your life.

God spoke to me about watching soap operas almost eighteen years ago. Now I only watch Christian TV programs. Even great secular programs are often disrupted by the garbage in commercials. We don't realize how easily things can defile our spirit. Our eyes and ears are the "gates" through which information, thoughts, and ideas enter. The Lord showed me how TV defiles the "eye gates" and the "ear gates." Many Christians will never be able to see or hear in the spirit realm because they have dulled their senses.

If you want to cleanse your eye and ear gates, pray this prayer with me:

"Lord, I give You permission to show me the things in my heart that are displeasing to You. Show me the things that are keeping me from going forward into all that You called me to do. Lord, I ask You to forgive me for anything ungodly that my eyes have looked upon. Cleanse my eye gates with the blood of Jesus. Lord, I repent of anything that my ears have listened to that was ungodly. I renounce all rebellion and unclean spirits that I have opened myself up to receiving. I take back all legal ground that the enemy had, and I give it to Jesus. Cleanse my ear gates with the blood of Jesus. I bind those spirits and command them to leave me now. Anoint my eyes and ears to receive from You. Fill me afresh with Your Holy Spirit. Thank You, Jesus, for setting me free."

An Angel In My House

I was alone at home, ironing and watching Joyce Meyer on TV. I sensed the presence of someone in the room with me, but I wasn't afraid. I looked up and saw a huge angel walking toward me. He was beautiful and tall. He had pure white woolly locks of hair, and a thick gold belt around his waist. There were gold epaulettes on his shoulders like royalty would wear. He had large fluffy white wings. They were visible above his shoulders and touched the floor.

His face was radiant.

The angel walked up to me and touched my left arm with the fingers of his right hand. He gently pushed his fingers into my skin. It felt as if I were being chosen by God for something special; it felt like he was marking me for the Lord.

I was amazed at the beauty of the angel and the presence of the Lord. I wondered, "Why is this angel visiting me in my house?" The angel turned around and started walking toward the foyer. As he was walking away I said, "You are welcome to stay here and protect me and my family." As he turned to go upstairs, he disappeared. I will never forget the feeling of when the angel touched me.

I never told anyone about this experience until two years later, when I met my pastor's mother, JoAnne, in New York. I was at her house when she started telling me how she sees angels. I felt so relieved that someone else had encountered angels and that I wasn't crazy. I told her about my visitation, excited that someone would understand what I had seen.

The Man On The Floor

A friend and I were shopping at the mall. We were walking through the jewelry department, and I noticed a lot of commotion over by the jewelry counter. There was a man lying on the floor. His white skin had a slight purplish cast, and his still body was outlined with red tape. It was obvious that he was dead. I heard someone say that this man hadn't had a pulse for quite some time. As soon as I saw him, the first thing that came to my mind was a testimony I'd heard R.W. Shambach, a healing evangelist, give on TBN just days before. He shared about praying over a dead man. He commanded the spirit to come back into the man's body and the man came back to life! The man was raised from the dead! I thought to myself, "If Shambach can do it, so can I."

I hurried over to where the dead man was lying. I stopped and knelt down to pray. I used the same words that I had just learned from Shambach. I stretched my hand toward him and commanded his spirit to come back to his body in the name of Jesus. The man's body started to shake and move, much to the amazement of my friend, the people standing around, and me! His color started returning to normal as the life came back into his body.

One of the store's cleaning women ran over to me and said in a strange demonic voice, "What do you think you are doing?!" I answered that I was praying for him. She said very hatefully, "Get out of here–NOW!" My friend started shaking and said, "Let's get out of here!" Then she turned to me and said, "What the hell did you just do? He was dead, but he looked like he was coming back to life! What did you do?" I said, "I just prayed for him and believed for the Lord to bring him back to life."

I was shopping in that store a few weeks later and saw that same man working behind the jewelry counter. It blessed me to know that he was back to work so soon. I knew God had spared his life.

A Family Upheaval

The next five years was the best "season" in my marriage to John. It was the only peaceful time for our family. There was no fighting or hitting. The boys loved their schools, had many friends, and were actively involved in sports. But a call from my husband changed everything. He told me he had just received a job offer in New York. The boys and I didn't want to move. We loved that area. I told him the only way I would go was if it were God's will. John said he wanted to go and just check it out. It was the only time we ever prayed together. I asked God, "If this is Your will, open the door. If it's not Your will, shut it." Little did I know this was the will of God, even though I was going to face one of the most difficult times in my life. The boys' friends didn't want us to move. They removed the realtor's "For Sale" sign and put it in the neighbors' front yard. It was a very difficult move for them, as well as for me.

The next thing I knew, we were moving to New York. I looked up at our house as we were backing out the driveway. I saw two rainbows over the house. I knew God was speaking to me. I didn't want to leave, but I knew I had to obey God. The rainbows spoke to me about restoration and promises that were mine. I had no idea of the "flood" that was ahead of me as we moved to New York, but I had a sign and a promise from God.

My older son was devastated: we had moved just before his senior year of high school. It broke his heart to leave his friends. This was one of the many things that made this an emotionally difficult time. As a Christian, I knew that if God had sent us there, then He must have had a plan. My children had just started at their new schools, and I became very depressed. I had never understood how people could get depressed; I had never experienced it before. I found myself crying and sleeping more than usual. I didn't know what to do with myself. Previously, I was always a homeroom mom at school or a volunteer at the church. But in my younger son's middle school, they didn't use homeroom moms.

Awards, Trophies, And Accomplishments

The first time we visited the Catholic Church, the priest asked me my maiden name. I thought it was very strange question. When I told him, he said my name wasn't welcome in that church. I was shocked how the priest treated me. I was furious as we walked to our car. In the church's parking lot, my son said to me, "Mom, I thought you were a Christian. You need to forgive him." I said, "You're right." I forgave the priest for his behavior, and we went back the next Sunday. Apparently, a man with the same last name had recently murdered a local girl, and the priest thought the murderer was my brother.

It was time to start all over again at that new church. I had nothing to do. My friends were gone. It seemed like the pattern of our marriage. Whenever we had built up a safe place, it was time to move again. I felt so bad for our children, moving from school to school. One year, Michael and Matthew attended three different schools for the same grade.

Despite the rough start, we stayed at that church, and I went on to become both a Eucharistic minister and a religious education teacher..

Our first week there I drove out to the plant where my husband worked as plant manager. I decorated his office with his awards and achievements that I had framed and saved for him. He also had awards and pictures from his years of coaching sports with our sons. I placed a family picture on his desk. The boys had even given him gifts for being a great dad. I wanted to make his office special for him.

Then I returned home to unpack and put up all the boys' many awards, achievements, and trophies for sports and academics. After I finished, I sat down on the top step of the stairs. I heard this voice say to me, "Where are your accomplishments and awards? What have you done with your life?" At that moment I felt so worthless. I came into agreement with that thought and a spirit of depression came on me. I kept thinking, "What have I done with my life?" The voice of the enemy started accusing me of all the things that I'd done wrong. The front door opened. It was Michael returning from school. He walked up the stairs where I was sitting crying and asked, "Mom, what's wrong?" I told him I had never known what depression was until now. He told me that he too was having a hard time being in a new school his senior year. Maybe I just needed to get out of the house.

Michael and I went to the mall the next day and were shopping at Old Navy when the manager walked up to me and asked me if I wanted a part-time job? He said, "You look like a cool mom. Would you be interested in working for us?" God was setting me up, and I didn't even know it. The manager gave me the job application and told me to take it home and think about it. I knew God was talking to me. It would be good for me to get out. After getting married, I hadn't worked many jobs. My husband had an excellent income, he didn't want me to work, and we both liked the idea of me staying home to raise our children. But, I felt good about taking this job. I needed something to do. I did not want to sit at home by myself. Soon I started working at Old Navy.

The Flood

Starting that new job was great. I enjoyed getting to meet my new co-workers. Tina was one of the employees that God used to changed my life forever. We always used to talk about the Lord. One day at work she said to me, "LuAnne, you always talk about the Lord. You love Him very much, don't you?" I said, "Yes I do." She said, "I really would love for you to come and visit our church. You talk about Benny Hinn all the time. If you like Benny Hinn, you would love our church, Mt. Zion Ministries." I thought to myself, "Why would I want to go to her church, when I have my own?" I didn't understand that I had a religious spirit that was trying to control me and keep me from the calling that God had for me. A religious spirit keeps you at the same place you are spiritually, or takes away what faith you have. It is based in pride and is unteachable. It takes away the desire to seek God with your whole heart. It is not open to truth, and it makes repentance and forgiveness almost impossible. Everyone has to keep a watchful guard against it.

Monday at work, Tina asked me if I would go with her to her church that night. I told her, "No. I have to teach the religious education class at the Catholic church tonight. I teach my son's class." She said, "I would love for you to come and hear a prophet from Washington state, Pastor Tracey Armstrong. He will be speaking tonight. You would love him. I really hope you can come." "I'm sorry, but I can't go. I really have to teach that class," I said. She replied, "Well, can't you get somebody to fill in for you?" "No," I said, "I want to teach it, it's my son's class."

I went home from work. I was getting ready to go teach when the phone rang. It was Tina! "LuAnne, God told me to call you and ask you one more time ... Can you come to the service tonight?" I held the phone at arm's length and said quietly, "What the hell is her problem?!" Then I brought the phone back to my mouth. "I told you I have to teach religion tonight!" Apologetically she said, "Well, I felt God told me to call and ask you just one more time. Okay. Goodbye."

As soon as I hung up, the phone rang again. It was the priest from the Catholic Church. He said, "Your catechism class is canceled tonight. I don't understand it. This has never happened in the seventy years that I have attended here. Your classroom has a water leak and your room is flooded. I've already called all of your students to cancel the class. There is no need for you to come tonight. Goodbye."

I started shaking. I knew this was God! As I hung up the phone, I thought, "God, you must really want me to go to the meeting with Tina. If this is You and You want me to be there, have my other friend from work, who is also Catholic, go with us." I thought it would be safe if I had another Catholic go with me. I called her up, and she said she would love to go. Her husband would not let her go anywhere, but that night he was out of town, even though he was seldom gone. She said she'd meet us there. We found it funny that the Lord made a way for her to go, so that I would also go.

I called Tina back and told her all that had happened. She was excited! She knew God wanted me to be at that service. As Tina and I walked into the church, I looked around and asked, "Where are the statues?" She said, "Oh, LuAnne, we don't use those here." I wondered if I should leave. Just then a woman came up to me and said, "I have a word from God for you. Would like to hear it?" I looked at Tina; she smiled and said, "It's okay, LuAnne." This woman, Rose, said, "The Lord says He wants to give you 100%, but you only have 50%. He's looking for you. And God says, 'Where are you?'"

Tears started streaming down my face. They asked me what was wrong. I looked at Tina and said, "I just prayed that prayer to the Lord this past Saturday night in the Catholic church. I said to the Lord those very same words. I said, 'Lord, I only feel 50% of You here. I want 100% of You. Where are You, Lord?'" I hadn't told anyone what I had prayed. I was amazed that the Lord had heard my prayer and the cry of my heart, word for word!

We went into the sanctuary to hear the prophet Tracey Armstrong speak. During the message he called all those who worked with children up to the front. I went up because I taught religion to the children at the Catholic church. He prayed that God would increase our anointing so we would touch children's lives for the Lord.

After I sat down, he started prophesying over a couple on the opposite side of the church. "Stand up," he said. "God is going to take you to the nations. You are going to lay hands on the sick and they shall recover. You are going to cast out demons, and you will raise the dead. God has an awesome ministry for you." As he was praying for that couple, he had his hands stretched out over their necks. My own neck began to shake uncontrollably. I looked over at Tina and asked her, "What's going on? Why is my neck shaking?" She said, "LuAnne, I believe that word is for you, too. The presence of God is all over you." I laughed to myself thinking, "Yeah, God, how am I going to go to the nations?" My mind couldn't comprehend that God could use me. I'd been a stay-at-home mom for most of my married life. Me, travel to the nations?

When I returned home that night, I lifted up both hands to heaven and cried out to the Lord, "Here I am. I am giving you 100%. Take me and use me. I'm yours."

Looking Under My Bed

The following morning, John had already left for work while I was still sleeping. The Lord woke me up at six thirty. I couldn't believe I was awake that early; normally I woke up at seven to get the boys off to school. I will never forget what happened next. Very clearly, I heard the word "Oriskany!" It was so loud that it startled me! I jumped out bed and looked under it. Then I looked in the closet. Where did that voice come from? I realized it was the audible voice of God. It was the first time God had ever spoken to me out loud. I ran downstairs and called my friend Tina. Even though it was early in the morning, I had to call her.

Tina could hear the tension in my voice and she asked me, "LuAnne, what's wrong?" "Tina," I replied, "I just heard God speak to me out loud!" She asked me, "What did He say?" I said, "Oriskany!" She said, "Oriskany? Why would He say that?" "I don't know," I replied. She said, "Let's pray and ask Him." "What?" I exclaimed! "Let's ask Him why he said that," she suggested. After she was done praying, she said, "LuAnne, would you like to come over to my house so we could pray together. You seem as if there are some things bothering you." I thought, "Why do I have to go over there? I don't want to go there." I asked, "Why don't you come over to my house?" She countered, "Why don't we meet halfway?" We agreed to meet at the Boulevard Diner.

I got Matt off to school and was getting ready to go meet Tina. As I was sitting on the stairs putting on my socks, suddenly, it dawned on me! The Boulevard Diner was on Oriskany Boulevard! As I walked into the diner and sat down at a table, I felt such a peace come on me. This was a divine appointment.

When she joined me, I shared my "discovery." "Tina, do you realize that this diner is on Oriskany Boulevard." Then I opened my heart and life to her. "Tina, I have to tell you something I've never told anyone before. I was sexually abused, and I had an abortion when I was eighteen. Can God forgive me?" I remember her response so clearly: "Jesus came to set the captives free! You are forgiven." At that moment it felt like a hundred pounds just fell off my shoulders. I felt such peace as my sins were forgiven and the hidden shame of abuse was broken. I had already confessed my sins when I received salvation but I had never confessed them to another believer, which brings healing to the brokenness. The Lord was just waiting for me to confess my sins so I could be healed and released from the oppression. Here are some scriptures that explain these truths:

"If we confess our sins, He is faithful and just to forgive us our sins and to cleanse us from all unrighteousness" (1 John 1:9).

"Confess your trespasses to one another, and pray for one another, that you may be healed" (James 5:16).

Tina and I had an awesome conversation about the Lord. I knew the hidden sin in my life brought shame that kept me from telling anyone. The shame also kept me from God. As a Catholic, I felt that abortion was the unforgivable sin, so I never had confessed it. I'd wondered if I would go to Hell, even though I served God in the church. As I drove home, the "war" began. "Did I do the right thing by telling Tina?" The enemy kept telling me I was an idiot! "Why did you tell her?" But I felt such a peace in my spirit; I knew I had done the right thing. I felt so clean and free. My conscience was clear. Unconfessed sin can bring depression.

Mary In The Trash

When I came home from the diner, I grabbed my rosary beads and started to pray the rosary as I sat in our living room chair. Then I heard the voice of God inside of me. It was the Holy Spirit speaking to me: "Turn in your Bible to John 14:6." I grabbed my Bible and starting flipping the pages. I knew the book of John was in there somewhere. I never read my Bible. It states, "I am the way, the truth, and the life. No one comes to the Father except through Me." "God, are you telling me not pray to Mary?" I fell to the floor on my knees begging God to forgive me for praying to Mary. He told me doing so was idolatry and necromancy, communicating with the dead. As I repented, I felt this band of pressure come off my head. It was a religious spirit that held me in deception to keep me from the full truth. I had such a revelation, I wanted to take it to the Pope!

I heard the Holy Spirit speak to me again, "I want you to throw out that statue of Mary." "God, how can I throw that statue out?" It was John's grandmother's statue; it had been passed down twice. "Lord, I can't throw it out. It's my husband's. If You want me to throw it out, John has to be okay with it." At that moment the telephone rang. It was John, calling from work. "Honey, what are you doing?," he asked. "Just cleaning the house," I replied. "What are you throwing out now?" he joked. I laughed when he asked that; I knew it was the Lord speaking to me through him. "Can I please throw out that statue of Mary? It's cracked anyway." He responded, "I don't care. I have to get back to work now. Bye." I knew God was making a way for me to destroy the idols that kept me in deception. I picked up the statue of Mary, put it in a plastic bag, and smashed it on the tile floor. I asked God to forgive me for necromancy and idolatry, and I commanded the religious and witchcraft spirits that had come into the house to leave.

As soon as I finished with Mary, the Lord said to me, "What about those other statues of saints?" I said, "Lord, forgive me for praying to them!" I went through the house and threw out all the saint statues and their accompanying prayer cards. I renounced all the prayers that I had prayed to Mary and the saints. My younger son used to put his prayer cards of Mary and the saints face-down before he went to sleep; he said they scared him.

At that moment I heard the voice of the Holy Spirit say, "LuAnne, throw out your Catholic Bible." I said, "Lord, what is wrong with the Catholic Bible?" He answered, "Turn to Revelation 22:18. No one should add to or take away from the word of God. They added eight books."

After I threw out the Catholic Bible, I searched the house to see if anything remained that was either a statue or a prayer card to the saints. The Catholic Church teaches that you can pray to the saints for favors. I know I used to pray to St. Anthony to find missing things. Later, I remembered a house where I had once buried an upside down statue of St. Joseph in the yard; doing so was supposed to help the house sell more quickly. I had to repent of that sin. I was trusting in something other than Jesus.

I had also thrown out my rosaries. But soon afterward, God gave me a dream in which I put my hand down behind the couch cushions and pulled out another rosary. I'd forgotten about. When I woke up the next morning, I ran downstairs and put my hand down the couch exactly where I did in the dream. Much to my surprise, I pulled out the same rosary I'd seen in the dream. God knew I had missed one! I was amazed of how God speaks to us even through dreams.

"God, You Saw That?"

At a later point, the Lord spoke to me clearly while I was vacuuming. "How about that china in your china cabinet?"

He said. "What about that china?" I asked. He responded, "You stole it." "God, you saw that? Lord, what are you saying?" I inquired. His answer surprised me: "I want you to throw it away." Shortly thereafter, Matthew came home from school. He turned to me and said, "Hey Mom, did God talk to you today?" I replied, "What! Why did you say that?" Matthew continued, "God always talks to you." I wondered what he said." I think Matthew could tell by the look on my face that God had spoken to me.

I told him the story. "I worked in a grocery store. They had china you could purchase with stamps given out as bonuses from buying groceries. Some people wouldn't save them, so I would take them. Some of the kids I worked with would put pieces to the set in my car. Some of it I bought, and some of it was stolen."

Matthew said, "Ma, you stole?" "Yes, I did, Matt." He walked over to the china cabinet, and removed a plate. After looking at it, he set it down on the table. He looked at me and said, "So this one you stole!" He reached into the china cabinet for another plate, and set it down next to the first one: "And this one you bought. How can you know which is which?" My thirteen-year-old son put his hands on his hips and replied, "Ma, what are you going to do? Some you stole, and some you paid for. You have to throw them all away. Does Dad know?" "No," I admitted. Matt replied, "You're going to have to tell him."

That day was John's birthday, and we went out to dinner to celebrate. During dinner, Matthew started kicking me under the table. "Mom, tell him, tell him," he insisted. John said, "Tell me what?" "You know that china in the china cabinet?" "Why? What's wrong?" he asked. "I stole some of it," I admitted. "The Lord told me to throw it away." John looked at me and said, "So throw it away." He never brought it up again. The next day I took the whole set to the dumpster and threw it away. God told me if I threw it away, He would give me new china. My china cabinet sat empty for ten years.

Years later, when I was going through counseling for abuse, I asked the church's pastor, Pastor Lon, "Why did I steal?" He said it is very common for abused people to steal because something so precious was stolen from them.

Dumping Daiquiris

One hot afternoon a friend came over to my house with some fresh fruit and alcohol to make frozen daiquiris. I liked sweet drinks, and had started drinking them in North Carolina before I was saved. I had seen the destruction that alcohol had done to my family. When I noticed that I was drinking them more frequently and starting to crave them, it scared me and I stopped. I was now walking with the Lord and had not drunk anything for some time.

I blended the drinks and poured them into glasses. I started to take a sip when I heard God speak to me clearly: "Pour it out now!" I looked at her and then looked at my drink. He repeated himself. Out of obedience I walked over to the sink and poured out my glass. She cried, "No! What are you doing?" I knew it was very important to obey God's voice. I had stopped drinking the first time because of the fear of destruction that could come with alcohol. This time I stopped because of my love for God and my desire to obey His every word.

When we do the right things for the right reasons, it produces a victory and "overcoming authority" in your life. Obedience in small things releases a stronger anointing for the greater challenges that lie ahead. David killed the lion and the bear before he faced Goliath. Take down your lion and bear now; Goliath will be yours as well!

It's Time To Leave

After I got rid of the Catholic saints that I prayed to, I found a greater desire for "more of God" than I was getting in the Catholic Church. God can use many things to draw you toward Himself, but when He shows you it's time to move on, you must go. Every time I went to mass with my family, I was very uncomfortable while I was there. But, I was waiting for the Lord to release me. The Bible tells us to seek the truth and that the truth will set us free. I was seeking the truth, and God was setting me free.

The Lord had given me a dream: he showed me that John was going into the Catholic church, and when I went to open the door behind him, it was locked. Matthew and I were standing outside. I woke up and asked the Lord, "What are You saying to me?" He responded, "I want you and Matt to leave this church and go to Mt. Zion Ministries." I replied, "Lord, I will go, but my husband has to release me." Later that day I prayed, then I went and asked John if he would be okay with Matt and me leaving the Catholic church and going to Mt. Zion. He said, "Honey, I know how you love the Lord, and if that is your desire, I'm fine with that."

John's response really shocked me! When he had asked me to marry him, he told me I needed to convert to Catholicism, which I did. At that time I was attending an Episcopal church. I'd had to take Pre-Cana marriage preparation classes (for Catholics) and be re-baptized into the Catholic Church before we could marry there. We had been married 20 years and never missed going to mass together. It was God's supernatural intervention that softened John's heart to release me to go to Mt. Zion. Afterward I told God, "I know You made a way, Lord, where there was no way." I knew the Lord intervened to release me.

Matt and I attended Mt. Zion Ministries for almost two years, while John attended the Catholic church. We would go to our separate churches Sunday morning; after church we would meet and have lunch together. When he could, Michael came home from college to visit us. John was okay with us not going to church together, but Michael was very upset with me. He didn't understand why we had raised him Catholic but now neither Matt nor I was attending the Catholic church.

During the two years I went to Mt. Zion Ministries, God was preparing me for the challenges I would soon face. After twenty-three years of marriage, my husband was about to leave me.

Me and my niece Bridget
on her birthday.

Matthew, just home
from the hospital with a
broken arm.

Me and Tina, who met me
at the diner in "Oriskany"
and set me free.

Chapter 4

Happy New Year

I t was New Year's Eve, and John had agreed to go to my church for the New Year's Eve service. As we were getting ready to leave, John told me that he wasn't going. I told him I wouldn't go either since the roads were snowy. He quickly responded that he would drive me there, but that he wouldn't stay for the service and would return home. While we were driving, Matt asked if he could go back home with his dad. I said that was fine. John got upset and tried to talk Matt into going to the church service. But Matt wouldn't change his mind. He dropped me off at the church, and Matt went home with his father. On the way home John told Matt he was stopping to get him some candy, but really he was going in to use the phone. When they arrived back at the house, Michael had come home from work. John was surprised that Michael was at home because Michael had planned on going to a friend's party. Michael was also surprised, as he knew his dad had planned on attending the church service with Matt and me.

The home phone rang, and John answered it. He said that he would be right there. After John hung up, he told the boys he had to go out to work. He claimed the security center had just called about an alarm going off at the plant. After John left, Michael picked up the phone and dialed a code to call back the last incoming number. He thought his dad was acting very suspiciously. The phone rang, and a woman answered it. It was the receptionist at the plant. Michael recognized her voice and said to her, "I don't know what your plans are with my Dad tonight, but they're not going to happen." Then he hung up. Michael was very upset and decided not to go to his friend's party.

John came to pick me up as soon as the service was over, right after midnight. As soon as I opened the SUV door, it felt like a knife went right through my heart. I knew something was wrong. John was acting weird. He told me that he didn't know what was wrong with Michael, but that Michael was very upset. When we went into the house, John went straight upstairs and went to bed. He never wished me a Happy New Year, or even talked to the boys. Michael said "I have to talk to you." He told me all about the phone calls. He told me that he thought his dad had gone to meet a woman who worked at the plant. I went up to our bedroom and turned on the light. John had the covers pulled over his head. I pulled the covers down so I could see his face. I asked him to please explain what he did that night. He said that he went to a party. "I asked him whom he went with." He said he went with a group of people from work. I found out later it was a lie. He had planned to meet this woman. I asked him about the woman on the phone. John stated that he had picked her up to take her to the party. Eventually it came out that he had been seeing her for a long time. God had given me dreams that John was seeing another woman, but he kept denying it. There was a battle in my mind. Was he telling the truth, was the enemy trying to torment me, or was God warning me? I was believing for the marriage to work, so I did not want to accept anything else.

The next day John stayed in the bedroom until early afternoon. When he came downstairs, Matt and I were talking at the kitchen table. John got down on his knees and begged for forgiveness over and over. I told him that I forgave him, but that we needed marriage counseling. After I forgave him, he said a "sinner's prayer" to accept the Lord. He agreed to go to church with me to talk with the pastors. He went to church with us for two weeks in a row. But after those two weeks, he walked out and said he was never going back again. I felt he was sorry he had been caught, but not for what he had done. It turned out that he continued his relationship with that woman from work.

I went to see his boss to tell him that John was seeing a woman at the plant. As I walked past the receptionist's desk, the desk of the woman with whom he was having an affair, I noticed a bouquet of roses. Valentine's Day had just passed, and John had given me red and white carnations. He knew how much I liked roses. Upon hearing my claims, John's boss was unsympathetic. "I can't help it if you can't keep your husband happy," he chided. "You better do something about it, or I will call your boss," I countered, and walked out of his office. Stopping into John's office, I noticed that the family picture had been taken off his desk—I found it facedown in a desk drawer. When I saw that, I knew our marriage was in trouble.

I went home and confronted John. "You bought her roses and me carnations." He denied the roses were from him, but I knew in my spirit that they were. The next day John had a dozen roses delivered to me. I took the roses and threw them in the garbage. He got mad, but I was breaking the cycle of control that he'd used in our abusive relationship, where gifts were used to appease me.

That week the receptionist stopped working there, and about a year later that general manager lost his job. Soon after that, the entire plant closed down. Truth has its own voice.

God will vindicate those He loves over time. Whatever you sow, you will reap.

The Golf Ball On My Table

As our marriage unravelled, God spoke to me regularly through dreams. Despite everything, I was still standing in faith for the restoration of our marriage. One night I had a very unusual dream: I was standing at my bedroom window looking at the end of the driveway. I saw a woman standing there, pointing a golf club at me. She yelled, "I am going to destroy you and this family." I opened the window and shouted back, "No you won't! I command you in the name of Jesus to get off my property." I woke up, startled by the dream. John had just left for work. I came downstairs and noticed a golf ball on my coffee table. This was very strange—it was the middle of winter, and it hadn't been there when I went to bed the night before.

After the dream I'd just had, it was very upsetting to see that golf ball lying there. I called my pastor's mother, who had a gift of understanding dreams. She said that she felt the woman represented a "spirit of Jezebel." She told me that I needed to grab that golf ball, open my front door, and throw it back at the enemy. She said, "Tell the enemy that you are not going to play his game in the name of Jesus." So, that is what I did!

The Fight

Those next several months were hell. John became more physically, verbally, and mentally abusive than ever before. He constantly denied he was seeing this other woman. I kept praying and believing for my marriage. John would continually make fun of me for what I believed and the church I attended. Often he would try to start a fight so he would have an excuse to leave the house. He started an argument about me leaving the Catholic church, even though he released me to do it. We were in the kitchen and I challenged him: "What, you think Saint Peter stands at the gate of heaven and says, 'Are you Catholic? Come in. No one else is allowed to enter heaven, only Catholics.'" John retorted, "This is what I think of you leaving the Catholic church"—and spat in my face. Immediately I responded, "I rebuke you in the name of Jesus!" and John ran out of the house. One day I received a phone call from one of the pastors at my church. He was very concerned for Matt and me. This pastor said that he believed John would hurt me, and that he had found a safe place for me to go to. I didn't believe it, so I stayed. Later that day, John started shoving me. He grabbed my shirt and then my hand. He shoved me into the refrigerator and then bent my hand backward to force me to the floor. It was very violent. I wasn't afraid, because he had done that many times before. However, Matt had never seen his dad abuse me until that day. When I went down on the kitchen floor, Matt ran toward us, leaped across the kitchen, and tackled his dad— the impact cracked three of John's ribs. Matt said to his dad, "If you ever touch my Mom again, I will kill you."

Matt and I got into the car and drove to my friend Tina's house. She and her husband were trying to talk me into not going back home. They were also trying to calm Matt down, who was very upset. We stayed with them for a couple of hours and then we went home. John had locked himself in the spare bedroom. The following morning he was nice to us again. It seemed as if we were back to "normal."

Suitcases Packed

On April 7, 2001, John took Matt and me out for breakfast that Saturday morning. While eating, we talked about picking up some homemade Easter chocolates after we took Matt to work. After we dropped Matt off, John started driving the opposite direction of the candy store, toward our home. I asked him where he was going. He answered, "I have to stop at home and pick something up." We drove home and he asked me to come inside for a minute.

I was in the kitchen while he was upstairs. When he came down, he had a suitcase in each hand. "What are you doing?" I asked. He set the suitcases down. "I'm leaving you," he announced. It felt like a knife stab to my heart. I was stunned. "What? Why?" He responded, "I don't love you anymore." Instinctively, I retorted, "I never loved you. But even if you don't love me anymore, do you understand what you're doing to our children?" He replied, "I don't care. If they knew what happened to me at eight years old, they would understand." I said "What!?" He picked up one suitcase and went out to the car. I picked up the other one and took it out to him; I didn't know if he would ever return.

I drove Matt to the church youth group meeting that Wednesday night. After I dropped him off, I went to the gym. Two hours later, I went back to the church and picked Matt up. When we drove into the garage, it was empty. We went in the house. Half of the furniture and most of John's things were gone. It was a weird feeling. The reality of the divorce started to hit me. Divorce feels like a tornado: everything is scattered and much is destroyed. I found out that John took all the money out of our bank account. I was talking with my friend, telling her what John had done. She told me that he could not do that. She said that she would call a lawyer friend and ask him about it. Afterward, she called me back with the information. Then I called John and told him that the lawyer informed me that he needed to put the money back, so he did.

I gathered eight bags of his clothes and other things that he left. He came by later to pick them up. I had left it all in the driveway. I didn't want him in the house. After he had loaded the car, I walked out to him and gave him a letter I had written him that morning. I said, "This is a note for you. I forgive you for everything you've done to us." He opened the letter and read it. It spoke of my forgiveness to him and my prayers that he would come to know Jesus. He folded it and put it in his shirt pocket. He tried to get me to sign the title of our Cadillac over to him so he could sell it. I told him that I wouldn't do anything until I talked with my lawyer. He got upset and left.

The phone rang. It was John. He said, "You are a nothing and a nobody, and you'll never be a somebody." I responded, "I'm a child of God, and that's all I care to be." Then I hung up. It rang again. He said the same thing. "You are a nothing and a nobody, and you'll never be a somebody." I answered as before: "I'm a child of God, and that's all I care to be." When I hung up that second time, the following thought occurred to me: "If he is telling me that I'm a nothing and a nobody, Satan must know I am going to be a somebody."

The Doorbell

Fear tried to grip me. How we were going to survive? I was terrified that my sons wouldn't have a father at home. Seven days after he left, he served me divorce papers. It was then I knew he had planned this all out long before leaving. I was on the phone praying with my friend Barb, when I saw a man walking up to the door swinging papers back and forth in front of him. He rang the doorbell. I took the phone with me as I answered the door. The man asked, "Are you LuAnne?" When I answered "Yes," he said, "Divorce papers for you." Barb could hear the man talking to me. She couldn't believe what was happening. I read the papers to see what the grounds for divorce were. These were the reasons listed:

1. I am divorcing her for being a born-again Christian.
2. All she watches is Christian television.
3. All she listens to is Christian music.
4. She is a zealot for God and will do anything for him.

I was blown away. I raised the papers up to the Lord and said, "Lord this is a declaration of who I am for You!" I was actually embarrassed for him. John didn't just come against me, but he also came against God. How could he attack my relationship with God in the divorce papers? The following scripture came to me: "Blessed are you when they revile and persecute you, and say all kinds of evil against you falsely for My sake" (Matthew 5:11).

At this time I was still believing God for our marriage to be restored because I knew how much a divorce would devastate our sons. During the abuse and hard times in our marriage, I wanted to leave, but I stayed for the sake of our children. In many ways John was a good father, but his explosive anger was very unpredictable. I knew the enemy wanted to destroy our marriage and our children. I prayed and interceded for our marriage for months after John left.

"Go To Your Room"

After returning home from a day of cleaning, I heard the Lord say to me, "Go to your bedroom, I need to talk to you." I thought, "Why do I have to go to my room for You to talk to me? Talk to me here." I walked over to the refrigerator and reached in to get a Diet Coke. The Lord spoke again, "I said, 'Go to your room!'" I knew it must be something very important He had to tell me; I was scared, yet excited. I went into my bedroom, shut the door, and lay on the bed. I didn't hear the Lord say anything more, so I started praying. Then I was quiet before the Lord. Finally He started talking to me. He said, "Let him go. Let him go. Let him go." I replied,

"God, You are not for divorce." He told me to let the marriage go because John's heart was hardened. The Lord said, "I will be your husband and I will be their father." He continued, "Read 1 Corinthians 7:15. 'If an unbeliever leaves, let him go.' Furthermore, if he is adulterous, it is grounds for divorce (Matthew 19:9)."

After reading those verses the phone rang; it was a woman who worked with my husband. "LuAnne, this is Barb. God spoke to me to call you and tell you that your husband is still seeing the receptionist who lost her job. God said that you needed to know the truth." I thanked her for calling and letting me know. As soon as I hung up the phone it rang again. It was my son Mike: "Mom, let Dad go. My friends saw him at the casino with his girlfriend." That phone call from my son released me to go forward with the divorce. My concern for my sons made it difficult for me to let go of the marriage, although there was little left at that point.

I called up John and told him, "I am letting the divorce go through. I am taking off my wedding rings. I release you." As I was speaking those words, I was literally removing my wedding rings after 23 years of marriage. I shared with John what the Lord had shown me from the scriptures and that I was released from the marriage according to God's word. I knew I had to trust God like never before; I had to believe Him for everything.

Anger In The Divorce

Divorce is a very painful experience. You feel unwanted. It is abandonment and rejection intensified by anger and hurts. If that ball of emotions is left to itself, it will develop into depression and worthlessness. Hatred and cynicism easily grip you. The emotions attached to divorce steal your identity. Divorce deforms the family. Furthermore, the impact on the children is devastating. It can bring anxiety, as well as a fear of relationships and marriage. During the divorce, our sons dealt with their feelings in different ways: Mike's anger resulted in black eyes for John. Matt, however, vented his feelings by kicking the Cadillac, resulting in two large dents. I am sure they shed tears that were never seen. I knew it was necessary for them to forgive John, as well as honor him as their dad, so that they would have the blessing mentioned in these scriptures:

"Honor your father and your mother, that your days may be long upon the land which the LORD your God is giving you" (Exodus 20:12).

"Judge not, that you be not judged" (Matthew 7:1).

Christmas used to be our family's favorite celebration. I would decorate the house from top to bottom. The first year of the divorce, Matt did not even want to put up the Christmas tree. Mike and Matt volunteered to be the security guards at the grocery store where they normally worked other positions in order to avoid being at home on Christmas day. For many years following, my sons limited their Christmas interaction with John to exchanging gifts in the apartment parking lot. However, their relationship with John is improving. I have always encouraged them to forgive him, yet not all the pain is gone for any of us. Healing is a process. Forgiveness starts with a choice. Be careful when you face pain in relationships, lest you become like the thing you hate.

First family picture as a single Mom

Chapter 5

"God, I Feel Like Cinderella!"

I got a call from my friend Tina; she asked if I would be interested in working for her daughter's cleaning business. I said, "Yes, I'd love to. I love to clean." I began cleaning houses with Tina's daughter. Shortly thereafter, the Lord told me through a prophet that he wanted to bless me with my own cleaning business. I really had a hard time believing this because I had such a fear of stepping out on my own. But, I got past the fear, and started my own business.

My first client was a friend. I was sweeping up the ashes in her fireplace when I became overwhelmed by my situation. I was now a single mom with a son in college and one at home. My house was in foreclosure and I was facing bankruptcy.

In frustration, I lifted my hands up to the Lord and cried out, "God, I feel like Cinderella!"

He answered me right away. He said, "You are Cinderella, and I will redeem you! I want you to name your cleaning business 'Cinderella's Cleaning Service.'" That night at church, a client from church I cleaned for said, "I feel that you should name your business." I laughed and said, "Yeah,

God already told me today!" I explained my "Cinderella" story." She loved it!

I was now cleaning the houses of my friends and neighbors. It was very hard and awkward, yet I was grateful. It was humiliating, but I was willing to do whatever it took to make ends meet. The church pastors whom I had known for several years—I was now their cleaning lady. It was easy for me to have a cleaning business, as my mom had taught me well. If I didn't do it right the first time, she made me do it over and over until it was perfect. I always enjoyed having an organized, clean house. People often commented on how nicely I kept my house, but I never imagined I'd be cleaning other people's houses for a living!

I never saw it coming. My husband had a high-salaried management position. If I wanted something, I would buy it. I went from "having it all," to having it all taken away. The things that weren't taken, I eventually gave away. I wanted nothing from my past. Later, the Lord even asked me to give away my expensive jewelry.

One time Matt and I didn't have any money and we needed bread. We gathered our Diet Coke bottles at our house and took them back to the store to buy bread. It was a very humbling experience. I learned to do what was necessary to make things work. I thought of the Bible story of the widow who didn't have money and was about to have her sons taken from her. She gathered all her bottles and vessels and then poured out the little oil she had for the miracle she needed. For years, I had volunteered at the food bank warehouse that our church ran. I never imagined that I would end up needing food from that very warehouse.

I carried a lot of shame and guilt through my life. The divorce added more. When you have been abused, you feel worthless. If you feel worthless, you feel hopeless. I had to carry my cleaning bucket across the street from where I lived to clean houses. God was breaking my pride. During the months I did not have a car, friends picked me (and my cleaning bucket) up to take me to work. Then someone else might take me to another house or business. At the end of the day, another person would drop me off again. I was afraid of running into my friends or neighbors—doing so meant having to explain everything that had happened to me. Every time someone would ask me about the family, John, or the divorce, all my pain and shame would resurface yet again. For too many years I worked hard at convincing everyone we were the perfect family. Now I had to tell the truth. The truth confused many people, but it was also a "reality check" for me.

One after another the Lord brought me more clients. I knew God was blessing my business. My business became my ministry as well. People I cleaned for witnessed God's goodness to me as I "walked through the fire."

You Were Always A Good Girl

In August, 2002, I was at church when Pastor Lon told me I needed to put aside what I was going through with my divorce and go visit my mom. She lived nearly six hours away, and was dying of cancer. Eight years prior, she had fought breast cancer. After surgery, she did very well, but now she had been struggling with bone cancer for two years.

I drove home with my sons to see her. We were shocked and brokenhearted to see how the cancer had ravaged her body. I knew that if God didn't heal her, she wouldn't have very long to live. It was hard for us to see her suffering. All that was left of her was skin and bones. She was very excited to see us.

The next morning I pushed her wheelchair into the living room. Her strength was gone. I felt God whisper, "Stop and tell her how thankful you are to have her as your mother. Ask her to forgive you for all the times you disobeyed her." After

I did that, she replied, "Honey, you never disobeyed me. You were always a good girl. You always listened to me." That was a special healing point with my mother. Growing up at home, I felt that I could never please her. She hugged me and we kissed.

We only had three days to spend together before I had to return home for work. I tried to make those days as special for her as I could. We spent as much time as possible talking with her. She slept a lot because of the painkillers. She asked me if I would take her for a drive, because she wanted to get ice cream cones for the boys. She pulled the vanity mirror down in the car. As frail as she was, she still had to put on her lipstick. Her hands were weak and unsteady–she ended up covering her lips and part of her face. The boys and I were caught between quiet laughter and tears. It was very hard to see her that weak. Later, at her funeral, Michael commented, "In her frailty, she still had her vanity." When it was time to leave, we prayed with her. She begged us not to go. We knew that it wasn't going to be long before the Lord took her home.

After I married Dale, Mike told me that before my mother died, she had asked the following of him: "Promise me that you will keep your mom and dad together." He agreed to it. I now understand how that promise produced false responsibility, pressure, anger, and frustration during the separation and divorce. I had Mike renounce that vow he had made to my mother, whom he had been very close to. It released a new peace to Mike.

The Doorbell Again!

After we returned to New York, my friend Freda visited me. We were getting ready to go to church when the doorbell rang. It was seven o'clock on Sunday morning! "Who could be at my door this early?" When I answered the door, the man there said, "I need the keys to your Jeep." I asked him why. He stated it was being repossessed. I replied, "That's not possible. My husband is responsible for the payments. It's written in the separation papers." He responded, "There is nothing I can do. I need to take the Jeep." I went to get my keys, and Freda ran upstairs crying. She couldn't believe how John was treating me. After the "repo man" left, I declared, "Satan, you have to return what you have stolen from me." I continued, "If you stole my Jeep, you have to return its worth sevenfold in this lifetime! I can't wait to see what God blesses me with!"

I had to get a ride from my friends to church, but I was praising the Lord. "The devil cannot take my joy!" Later I prayed, "God, how am I supposed to get a car?" I had no money. My husband had destroyed my credit by declaring bankruptcy, forcing me to do the same. But I knew that my God would supply all of my needs according to His riches in glory by Christ Jesus (Phillipians 4:19).

My friends from my prayer group, Cathleen, Kim and Mike, came over and announced they intended to take me to a car dealership. They said, "LuAnne, you need to pick out the car that you want and claim it from the Lord. The enemy stole your car, and we are in agreement that God will restore a better one to you. What kind of car do you want?" I told them I wanted a BMW. "A BMW!?" they replied. "Yes," I said, "a BMW!" So, we drove to a BMW dealership in Utica, New York. I informed the salesman I was interested in the BMW 7 Series and asked for a brochure. After he had gone back into the dealership, I went over to the 7 Series, laid my hands on it, and prayed this prayer: "In the name of Jesus, I thank You, Lord, that what the enemy stole from me You are going to restore. I thank You for this BMW that You have for me in the name of Jesus. Amen."

I went home, cut out the picture of that BMW 7 series, and put it on my refrigerator. This was before we were evicted out of our home. For two years it was on my refrigerator. My sons asked me why I had a picture of a BMW on the refrigerator. I told them I was believing God for a BMW. They laughed at me and sometimes made fun of me. They thought I was crazy to believe God for something that expensive when I had nothing. Thinking back to this part of my story made me cry. Other people who were close to me also didn't believe I was hearing from God as He directed the many steps in my life. At times it was hurtful and frustrating. God wants to know if you'll listen to His voice more than the voices of others. I told anyone who asked about the picture of the BMW that what the enemy stole from me, he had to give back sevenfold.

The Power Of Forgiveness

Later that week I received a phone call from a church friend, Frank Mellace, who was also my divorce lawyer. "LuAnne, how is your mother doing?" he inquired. "She is not doing well at all." I replied. "LuAnne, is she saved?" "Frank, she said the prayer to receive Jesus as her Lord and Savior, but she told me that she still harbors unforgiveness in her heart." I had explained to her how important forgiveness is, but she said that she could never forgive certain people. I told Frank that there were three people who had hurt her whom she hadn't forgiven. "LuAnne," Frank said, "hang up the phone and call her right now. Tell her she has to forgive those people. If she doesn't forgive them, God can't forgive her." Matthew 6:14–15 illustrates this clearly: "If you forgive those who sin against you, your heavenly Father will forgive you. But if you refuse to forgive others, your Father will not forgive your sins" (New Living Translation).

So I hung up the phone. I prayed, "Jesus, I plead Your blood over this next conversation with my mom. I bind you, Satan, in the name of Jesus. You will allow her to speak to me. I command you, Satan, to be subject and silent. I thank You, Lord, that my mom will be alert enough to talk to me."

Then I called my mom. I knew she had been slipping in and out of a comatose state the past few days. My dad answered the phone. "Dad, how's Mom?" I asked. He replied, "She hasn't been responding, but she just woke up!" My mom said, "Jack, who is on the phone?" "LuLu," he replied. My mom said she wanted to talk with me.

My dad was amazed that she was so alert. We talked for a bit, then I said, "Mom," I said, "Jesus wants to heal you or take you home. But you need to forgive those who hurt you. Will you forgive them?" I asked her. After a few seconds she responded, "Yes, I forgive. I forgive, I forgive." She named the three people and forgave them. I said, "Now Jesus can forgive you." Then the phone slipped from her hands and hit the floor as she went back into a comatose state. I rejoiced when I hung up, knowing she'd finally released her unforgiveness. That was the last time I talked with her. She died the next morning at eight o'clock, and I got a call from my father saying she had just passed away. I actually rejoiced, because she was no longer suffering. I was excited to know she was with my Lord and Savior, Jesus Christ.

How much more could I handle? The scripture came to me that God does not give anyone more than they can bear. What he takes you to, he takes you through. My mother had passed away and I didn't even have a car to go to her funeral! The funeral home was a five-hour drive away. One of the clients that I cleaned for ran a car business. The owners, Roger and Mary, allowed me to drive one of their cars to her funeral. This was just another away of God's provision through his people. I will always be grateful for their generosity.

I met my father at the funeral home. I put my arms around him and simply held him. He was very sad. He loved my mother. The funeral was held in a church, and I asked the staff to play the song "I Can Only Imagine" during part of the ceremony. The song speaks of meeting Jesus in heaven for the first time. I raised my hands as they played the song, rejoicing that she was with the Lord and not in pain any more.

Michael spoke at her funeral. The title of his eulogy was "Don't Be Afraid." He talked about the things my mom had feared. Her biggest fear was dying. His last words to her were, "Mimi, don't be afraid." His eulogy was very touching, and brought the family to tears.

My brothers and sisters seemed so sad. They said they couldn't believe how happy I was in spite of all of the things that I'd been going through. I shared how God had provided for all of my needs, even through the losses. God gives peace and comfort to those who mourn. My siblings said they were very proud of me. Right after I returned home from the funeral, I received papers that our home was going into foreclosure. I felt like Job in the Bible...

It's Time To Travel

Less than two months later, Frank said to me, "LuAnne, you need to go on a mission trip to Brazil." He had just returned from a trip to Brazil with Randy Clark, a healing evangelist who trains Christians through international ministry trips. Frank said the trip had been a powerful experience. I laughed at him and I said, "How could I go to Brazil? I'm losing my home. I don't have a car. I just lost my mom, and I'm going through a divorce." I couldn't even fathom going to Brazil, let alone the money it would cost to get there. Little did I know that it was a prophetic word. God was speaking to me.

I had been a stay-at-home-mom for many years. I was eighteen years old before I had ever been to the ocean. The idea of going on a mission trip to Brazil, or any other nation, was not on my agenda. It seems God had a different agenda.

It was hard for me to shift my mindset. I was losing every-thing, yet I was supposed to do something I'd never done before. The prophetic word that Prophet Tracey Armstrong spoke over the couple about going to the nations, that caused my neck to shake uncontrollably, was now coming to pass for me.

Our church held a conference and I was working at the book table. A friend named Kathy walked up and threw a check down on the table. I asked her what it was for. She turned around as she kept on walking and said, "I don't know. Ask God. He told me to give it to you." I thanked her. I looked down at the check and saw it was for $100. As I was looking at it, the Lord explained, "This is a down payment for Brazil." I laughed out loud. "Yeah, right. How am I going to go to Brazil when I don't even have a car?" I argued. At that moment a man from Rhode Island walked over to the table and handed me a $100 bill. "God just spoke to me to give this to you," he expressed. Then I heard the Lord say to me, "This is the rest of your down payment." The down pay-ment for going on Randy Clark's next mission trip to Brazil was $200. I was surprised at how quickly the Lord brought it to me.

The next morning was our regular Sunday-morning ser-vice. Pastor Lon walked up to me and said, "Hey, LuAnne. I believe you're supposed to go to Brazil." Pastor Lon did not even know about the money that had been given to me. I laughed and said to him, "Okay, if this is God, have Pastor Mike come and tell me I'm supposed to go to Brazil." During worship, Pastor Mike walked up to me and quietly said, "LuAnne, the Lord told me that you were supposed to go to Brazil. Sister Barb (his wife) and I are giving you $250." I started to cry. "Okay, God, I'll go. But I need more money." The money kept coming in week after week.

I went to the passport agency with two of my friends, Tina and Carleen. We were told our passports would arrive in the mail in three-week's time. Theirs were delivered as expected. Mine, however, hadn't arrived. I waited another week, thinking it would arrive any day. The following phone call was unforgettable. As I was walking toward the ringing phone, the Lord spoke to me clearly. He assured me, "Don't worry. I have everything under control." I thought, "What do you mean, God?"

The caller was a woman from the passport agency. She said, "LuAnne, the money you paid for your passport was stolen, and the thief destroyed your birth certificate and identification documents." She told me that if I called the records office in Albany, they would create a new birth certificate which would then be sent to the passport agency in Utica. From there, the birth certificate and passport would be sent to the Brazilian Embassy in Washington, D.C. They would issue the needed visa and would FedEx everything back to me. Given the departure date, the woman said it would take a miracle to get my passport in time.

So, I just believed and trusted God that He would take care of the situation. It was Friday, the day before we were leaving for Brazil, and my passport still hadn't arrived. I was looking out my front door, waiting for Tina to come over. She was coming over to pray for me concerning the trip to Brazil. I saw a FedEx truck coming down the street; Tina was following right behind it. She was so excited! She knew it was going to be my passport. Sure enough, it was! It came just in time. It's amazing how God provides for us, but I had to trust Him for everything. All of the trip money had come in. My sons found it hard to grasp that I was really going to Brazil when I didn't even own a car! The next day the team from our church flew to Houston where we met the rest of the ministry team, who flew in from other states.

We arrived in São Paulo, Brazil; I was very excited, anticipating what God was going to do. From there, we spent three days in Recife. After the first meeting, teams were released to pray for people. The first person I prayed for was a bitter, hard-hearted man who wouldn't forgive his wife for something she did thirty years ago. As I shared my story with him, tears formed in his eyes as the Lord softened his heart. "Life isn't fair," he said. I told him, "We all go through things that are hurtful, and most of the time it comes from people who are the closest to us." That broke something in him. He said, "Okay, I will forgive her." When he forgave his wife, the hardness fell off of him. Tears started to flow down his cheeks. He said he felt such a release when he forgave her. It was thirty years of hardness that had been nurtured by holding on to the hurt and pain.

After I ministered to him, seven women were brought over to me for prayer. Every one of them was, or had been in an abusive marriage. Some were divorced. Others, their husbands had abandoned them. One woman said to me, "I'm divorced. My husband left me. I'm depressed. Would you agree for God to do a miracle?" I shared my testimony with her. I told her, "You need to look to God and not to man for provision." I told her how worshiping God had kept depression away for me.

When you go through divorce, the enemy makes you feel as if you are not wanted. There is such a spirit of abandonment and rejection that tries to stay on you. You feel that there is something wrong with you, even though your spouse ended the marriage. You have to battle with self-hatred, loneliness, and depression. Isolation can seem safer, but it brings more depression. After getting divorced, you feel like you wear a big "D" stamped on your forehead. I had a hard time believing God could use me in ministry after being divorced.

As I started to pray for these women, I could feel the weight of rejection and abandonment fall off of them. The enemy creates spiritual strongholds out of places of hurt to rule your life. He tries to keep the hurts alive so that it will feed the spiritual strongholds. Spiritual strongholds use the past to block your future, creating a sense of hopelessness.

My pastor was watching as I prayed for these women. He saw them weeping as the strongholds in their lives were broken. Amazed, he said, "LuAnne, do you now realize the call that is on your life? What you came out of and got victory over, God is using to minister to others. Whatever you get victory over, God will use it to help others."

Rain Drops Falling On My Head

The next city we went to was Joao Pesseo. There was a tremendous outpouring of miracles. I was amazed at the Brazilian people's faith for miracles. I kept thinking of Hebrews 11:6, "But without faith *it is* impossible to please [God]." They had lots of faith.

After Joao Pesseo, we went to Natal, where the meetings were held in a very large indoor arena. There were at least 3000 people there. Davi Silva and Mike Shea led worship. Davi had a tremendous anointing in worship, healing, and signs and wonders. Randy Clark was the speaker. He was talking about how "God can use 'little old me.'" He said, "God is getting ready to take some of you into a supernatural experience. But you need to repent of anything in your way that would keep you from what God has for you."

The thought came to me that he was also speaking to the ministry team, not just to the people attending. He continued, "Ask the Holy Spirit to show you if there is anything you need to repent of and ask forgiveness for ... There are some of you here who have repented and are feeling raindrops." I remember the Holy Spirit said to me, "You need to repent of pride." I immediately repented. As I did, I felt rain drops falling down on me! But there was a ceiling over me! I could not understand where the rain was coming from. At that moment, Kathi Oates, who was one of the speakers, turned around and said to me, "Girl, get up here. God is getting ready to do something awesome with you."

I ran up to the front. Immediately I fell over under the power of God. I stayed "under" for at least twenty minutes. My whole body was shaking because of the presence and power of God. Randy Clark said, "Don't worry about what these people are doing on the floor. God is taking them into an awesome experience. I've seen people who get touched by God like this go on to be used in ministry for the Lord because they've repented."

I was not aware of my surroundings. I was having an awesome visitation from the Lord. I went into an open vision. I looked in awe as I saw bones lying in the dirt. Flesh starting to appear on the bones. It was an African man. He came back to life while I was watching! This man was just raised from the dead in front of me. I heard the Lord speak to me clearly, "You are going to raise the dead."

As I came out of the vision, I tried to stand up. But the power of God was so strong, standing was very difficult to do. My pastor walked toward me as I was getting up. "What's going on?" Pastor Mike asked. "I just had a vision of a man raised from the dead." As soon as I said that, the power of God hit him. It literally threw him backwards. "I believe you, I believe you!" he proclaimed. At that moment Davi, the worship leader, came up with a translator and said he needed to talk with the woman who had been lying on the floor. He explained, "I need to share with her what I saw in the spirit realm as she was on the floor."

He saw twelve angels standing around me. Six of them were rolling me over the map of Brazil. He went on: "I see you going into a morgue in Brazil ... You are going to raise the dead." When he said that, I started to shake uncontrollably again. He continued, "God is giving you the power to raise the dead. The other six angels were placing shiny mantles on your shoulders. Each mantle is a higher level with the

Lord. You are going to do many great things in the Lord. You also see in the spirit. You see angels?" I replied, "Yes, I do."

I had such an awesome encounter with God in Natal, Brazil. Now I understood why the devil didn't want me to have a passport. He knew that God had a divine appointment for me in Brazil. As I was returning home, I knew I would never be the same again. I was so on fire for God. I felt nothing could stop me from going after all that God had for me. I understood why the devil had used John to do the things he had done to us. Satan will do anything he can to stop you from going into your destiny. The enemy will even use the closest people around you to stop you from going forward in what God has for you.

A Check In The Mail

The goodness of the Lord provided for me and met all of my needs throughout my abandonment, rejection, pain, and abuse. The following August someone sent a letter to Pastor Mike with a check for me to go back to Brazil. It was my second trip with Randy Clark and Global Awakening. During a meeting, an American pastor named Rick Sodmont stood up and shared that during worship God had taken him up to heaven and had shown him a vision. "God, I want to have an experience like Rick had," I said. The Lord did many great miracles, signs and wonders on that trip.

The following November, I got another check in the mail with half the down payment to go to Africa with Global Awakening. The week before we were to leave I only had half of the money. I called Global Awakening to inform them that I would not be able to go. They said, "We know you're destined to go. Keep believing God, and the rest of the money will be there when you return." So, I went on my third trip. This one was to Ghana.

After one meeting Gary Oates, a team leader, asked if we would like to go out into the village to pray for people and the children. As we walked through the village, I was stunned to see the small huts and the hardship in which the people were living. But the people were so friendly. We prayed for many villagers, and God touched them with awesome healings, signs, and wonders. At another meeting Gary asked if a team member and I would pray for the children. That night 110 children gave their lives to the Lord and were filled with the Holy Spirit. Another night we were in the middle of the meeting when the enemy turned out all the electricity, but as soon as we prayed, God brought it right back on.

We were loading up onto the bus after a meeting, and I heard the people talking about the bus not starting. I looked at Frank and said, "This is witchcraft. Let's go pray with the driver for the bus." I asked Gary if it was okay, and he said yes. We walked up to the bus driver, and I put my hand on his back. I asked him to put the key in the ignition, but he insisted, "No, no, no. It won't start." I asked him again to put the key in the ignition, and finally he did. I commanded the bus to start in the name of Jesus Christ. At that exact second the bus started and everybody started clapping. It was such a victory! We broke the witchcraft that was sent against us.

A few hours later, we stopped at a convenience store. Some friends began yelling, "LuAnne, look. Look!" There was a car that wouldn't start; four guys were pushing it and trying to get the engine to turn over. The thought came to me, "Can God do it again?" The Lord rebuked me and said, "Why not?" I stretched my hand toward the car, but turned my head away because I didn't want to look. As soon as I said, "In the name of Jesus Christ I command that car to start," it did! The guys jumped in, and took off down the road. My friends were shouting, "Look! It started!" I asked God to forgive me for not believing that He could do it again. I was amazed at the power God has given us.

After the preaching that night, it was time for us to minister to those who wanted prayer. A woman was brought to my prayer line, and several of her friends explained her situation to me. This woman had not spoken in three years. I asked what had happened three years ago. Her friends said she went to a witch doctor, who was also a midwife, to have her baby delivered. I put my hand on her throat and commanded the spirit of witchcraft demons that were holding her voice to release it in the name of Jesus Christ. At that very moment the woman shouted, "Jesus! Jesus! Jesus!" She kept on shouting "Jesus." Her friends were so excited to see the miracle and to hear her voice after three years. I told her that curses come upon those who go to witch doctors. I also prayed for a man who was deaf in one ear, and God restored his hearing. It was amazing to see the Lord do so many healings and miraculous things.

On this trip we ate was chicken and rice every single day. Sometimes they would change it to rice and chicken! I started complaining because I don't like rice, and that's all they had. I wanted some American food, and said how much I would love a peanut butter sandwich. Rick advised if I would stop complaining, God would answer my prayer. As soon as I repented, God answered. The team was going back to the hotel before the next service. On the way back Frank was telling Rick about how he always brings peanut butter on these international trips because he didn't care for the local food. I said, "Peanut butter! I want some." Frank said he had two jars in his suitcase and that I could have one. God answered my prayers so quickly after I repented. Our trip to Ghana was powerful. Upon returning, I received a phone call that the rest of the trip had been paid in full! I was amazed God had sent me on three international trips within twelve months—and He paid for all of them.

Not too long after returning from Ghana, I was cleaning a friend's house. I was talking with her when her husband came home from work. He worked for a national nonprofit organization. He asked me if I knew John Smith. I answered, "Yes, that's my husband. Why?" He responded, "He just donated a Cadillac to our foundation." "That was our car," I sighed. It hurt to know John had my Jeep repossessed, then had given away our car, all while buying a nice SUV for himself.

Months later I was able to buy a used Jeep. From cleaning, I had managed to save up three thousand dollars. In addition, a friend had loaned me two thousand dollars. The bankruptcy ruined my credit, so I had to pay cash. I finally had a vehicle after ten months. I thank God for all my friends who gave me rides during those ten months. It felt like I was starting to get back a normal life.

The Eviction

When the eviction papers came, my son Matt and I had to leave the house. God spoke to me to believe Him for a miracle. When the house went into foreclosure, I didn't pack a thing. God told me not to pack, nor to prepare to move the day of the foreclosure. I believed God for a miracle. Pastor Lon had called and said, "LuAnne, I believe that God spoke to you, and I'm in agreement for your miracle." The phone call came. The realtors informed me the house had sold. I waited to see what God was going to do. Soon after, the new owner came to my door and introduced herself. "I just bought this house," she said. "I don't know why I went to the foreclosure, but I felt that God sent me." She said she was a Christian, and then stated, "I heard your story and I want to help you to stay in the house." We agreed on a monthly rent of $750.

God told me He was going to keep me in the house, and He did. But three months later, the new owner sent me an eviction notice because she wanted $2000 a month for rent.

We went to court. The judge hearing the case was named Judge Christ. I couldn't keep from laughing. I knew God was telling me that He was for me. When our case was called, the judge asked the owner, "What are you renting, the Taj Mahal? Why are you asking for so much money?"

The woman wouldn't change her mind, and I was given three days to move out. I thought, "God, I don't understand this, but I am trusting in You." I started packing all of my things, but I had no idea where I would go. No one would take me because of the bankruptcy and the foreclosure, but I kept on believing God was going to come through for me. Little did I know that God was moving me toward my restoration.

I donated my refrigerator and stove to the food warehouse that Mt. Zion Ministries owned. They gave food to the poor and to many other assisting organizations. As I removed the picture of the BMW that I had placed in faith on my refrigerator, my son Mike commented, "Yeah, right. You're asking God for a f---ing BMW and you just lost your f---ing home." I took that picture and placed it in my Bible at Matthew 19:26, "With God all things are possible." I kept that picture in my Bible for five more years. When they saw it, people would ask me about it, at which point I would share my story and my faith.

That Sunday morning, September 19, 2004, was our last day in that house. It was a very difficult day. God always shows His goodness by the way He does things. The day I lost my house in New York was the same day He gave me my new house in Delaware five years later. When Dale and I were married, he moved out of his house and we moved into an RV down at the beach. We wanted "all things new" (Revelation 21:5). On September 19, 2009, we moved into our new house. That first night in our new home, it occurred to me that it was the same day I left my last house. Wow!

Back to my current situation: We had no place to sleep that night. As we left for church, with all our belongings tucked away in storage, Matthew said to me, "Mom, don't look back at what we came out of, but look forward to what God is going to do with us." I thanked the Lord for an awesome son who had great faith. I was emotionally overwhelmed, and it was difficult drive to the church. I kept thinking, "Where are we going to sleep tonight?"

We arrived at church; the worship service had just started. Matthew walked to the front of the church as I was going to the intercessors' room. I watched him standing at the altar with his hands lifted up, worshiping the Lord. Tears came to my eyes. We didn't even know where we were going to sleep that night, but he was still worshiping God! I walked into the intercessors' room and started to pray. As we prayed, Pastor Mike said, "Someone here needs to give God the glory." I took a step forward, lifted my hands to the Lord, and proclaimed, "Though they slay me, I will praise Thee."

At that moment, a friend walked up and said to me, "LuAnne, do you need a place to stay? We just bought a home, but we will not be moving into it for thirty days. You and Matt are welcome to stay there." If you put your trust in God, He will provide your every need. After intercession I walked to the front of the church where Matt was still worshipping. "Matt," I said, "Kathy and Mark just gave us their home to live in for 30 days. God provided again." He looked at me and asserted, "Mom, I knew God would come through. He always provides for our every need. He is so faithful."

Later that year I was driving to work and listening to K-LOVE (a popular Christian radio station) interview a homeless woman. She called in for prayer for a home. She asked, "Is there anyone out there that didn't know where you were going to sleep that night?" Tears came to my eyes as I felt her heartfelt prayers. I remembered that day. The Lord spoke to me and said, "I allowed you to feel what it is like to be homeless so that you can minister faith to them."

Staying at Kathy and Mark's home was awesome. It felt like such a safe place, and showed God's love for us. But I kept wondering with excitement what God was going to do for us next. During that month I kept looking for a place to stay, but the bankruptcy had destroyed my credit rating. As the thirty days came to an end, we had to move. Right before we had to leave that house, I received a phone call about a cleaning job for a business office. This company also owned an apartment complex in Clinton, New York, only five miles from where we lived. When we met, I shared my story with them. They hired me to clean for them, and also said I could lease an apartment that had just opened up. I was so excited to have my own place! Soon I was able to save up enough money to buy some new furniture. It was amazing to watch God at work in my life. Obedience and faith were two major keys for releasing the supernatural in my life. I was in that apartment for more than two years.

It was great having my own place. But even in that joy, the enemy tried to shove me back down again. The very first week in that apartment, a letter came from the local Catholic diocese. I opened it, and was astounded to learn the diocese was annulling our twenty-three-year marriage. It felt like a slap in the face. How could they annul my marriage when my husband had left me and was living with another woman? I threw the letter down on the table, wondering what else John could possible do to us. Matt was standing in the kitchen with me. He asked, "What's wrong, Mom?" I told him it about the annulment. Matt picked the letter and read it. He, too, threw that letter back down on the table and stated, "That makes me a bastard son." He was very hurt. I was surprised that he thought of it.

Michael and me at his college graduation.

Freda was with me when my Jeep was repossessed.

Mark and Kathy gave us a place to live when we were homeless.

With friends in Brazil.

Me and Bunnie.

Chapter 6

Under The Apple Tree

I was attending a conference at Airport Christian Fellowship in Toronto. During the ministry time I received a prophetic word that I was not expecting: "Something happened to you as a little girl, some sort of abuse. The Lord says to tell you that He was with you when you were under the apple tree crying. The Lord is taking off all the fear, stress, and trauma that was put on you."

When I returned home from the conference, I had a dream. In it, I was standing in my apartment kitchen. A little girl with dark hair came around the corner. She looked at me with tears in her eyes. She had wet herself. I could see the shame on her downcast face. I asked her if she had wet the bed, but she was afraid to tell me. She ran past me to the large cabinet under the kitchen sink, opened the door and climbed inside, and shut the door to hide.

When I woke up I asked the Lord who the little girl was; He responded that it was me, and she had wet herself because she had been defiled by others—creating fear, shame, guilt, and condemnation. The little girl in me was still in hiding.

That morning I went to work thinking about the word the Lord spoke to me in Toronto and the dream I had just

99

had. The more I thought about it, the more pain it brought to me. The Lord was moving me into a place where I was very uncomfortable. I tried not to think about it, but He kept speaking to that issue. When I returned home, I opened the mail. There was a letter from someone I had not heard from in a long time. Enclosed was a framed picture of some of my siblings and me that had been taken on the very same day I'd been raped as a child. I felt the anger from inside of me start to boil up. I threw the picture against the wall, shattering the glass. I yelled at God, "I don't want to deal with this place. It's too painful!" The Lord knew what I had been through and how it had wounded me. He wanted me whole.

When I was nine years old, a person whom I trusted said that he had some candy for me and asked me to go for a walk with him in the woods. We walked for a long time. Then he tore my clothes off and raped me under an apple tree. Afterward, he ran off and left me lying there alone. I was utterly frantic because of what had just happened, and also because I didn't know how to get home. I put my clothes back on and ran for home. Eventually I made it back, tears streaming down my face, quietly sobbing. I hated myself for believing his lie; I also hated myself because of the shame which that abuse put on me. It made me feel so dirty. After stumbling back to my house, I took a hot bath—I scrubbed myself over and over again—I just couldn't get clean. I could not wash the away the shame. Growing up with that horrible secret was like being locked in a closest and not being able to breathe. That shame covered me everywhere I went; it was always with me.

He had lied, abused, and abandoned me. It destroyed my trust, and has made it difficult for me to get close to people. I started to believe that people would always hurt me; it produced a stronghold in my life. A "bitter root expectation" was planted in my childhood; I believed that anyone I became close to would abuse me. When you think this way, it opens the door for more pain and abuse into your life. It took my joy away and released anger inside of me.

If you are not rooted and grounded in love, it is impossible to believe that you are loved or can be loved. I was rooted in the shame and pain of abuse. I had a hard time loving until Christ came into my heart. There were so many other people who had walked over my heart and hardened it. I was a prisoner to those experiences, but Christ was the key to unlocking the prison doors. Each day is a process of growing in love. For an abused person, pain feels more normal than love. Love seems like a fantasy.

"For this reason I bow my knees to the Father of our Lord Jesus Christ, from whom the whole family in heaven and earth is named, that He would grant you, according to the riches of His glory, to be strengthened with might through His Spirit in the inner man, that Christ may dwell in your hearts through faith; that you, being rooted and grounded in love, may be able to comprehend with all the saints what is the width and length and depth and height—to know the love of Christ which passes knowledge; that you may be filled with all the fullness of God" (Ephesians 3:14–19).

Apple Blossom Drive

We had finished the manuscript for the book. Dale asked me again if I would consider putting in the story about the apple tree. I told him that it was my book and I did not want it in there. Each time I would talk about it, tears would come to my eyes. As we lay in bed that night, Dale said that he kept prophetically hearing the words "shattered expectations" for me. The next morning Dale encouraged me again to put the apple tree story in the book. He told me that it was a very important component to the book, and a key for many others to be healed. I finally agreed, and he started typing the story as I told it. As he typed the words *"shattering the glass,"* I had an epiphany—the stronghold was shattered in my life! Simultaneously, there was a first loud crack of thunder that sounded as if it were right inside the house. I yelled, "Jesus!" as I jumped from the kitchen barstool into Dale's lap. It seemed like God was confirming Dale's thoughts. Dale said the scripture came to him where Jesus says, "I saw Satan fall like lightning" (Luke 10:18). I had been freed from that stronghold.

With the story now finished, we tried to upload the manuscript to the publisher's website. But, somehow we couldn't get it to work correctly. We were on our way to Texas to see Dale's two youngest sons, and we knew his son Andrew could help us. Sure enough, he did, and after they left for work we went to Cracker Barrel to celebrate the manuscript's completion.

During the meal, I was still not at total peace about that story. Dale told me it was an important part of the book. As we were leaving, I glanced into the gift shop. A large plate on display featured these words:

With a heart that is true
I'll be waiting for you
In the shade of the old
Apple Tree.

I stopped in my tracks—I knew God was speaking to me. I grabbed Dale by his arm and said, "Why would anyone write that?" Tears came to my eyes. I knew that God wanted to take me back to that place to bring healing. He was waiting for me.

That night when I went to bed, God asked me, "What is your address?" Puzzled, I answered, "299 Apple Blossom Drive." God responded, "I gave you this house, and I am 'double blessing' you to break what the enemy did to you at nine years old. It is your time to blossom." God knew that part of me was still living in pain under the shadow of that apple tree. The Lord does not want our past to hold our future hostage. It is crucial to expose the enemy, and break the lies of shame. How awesome is our God!

The Little Girl Who Stuck Out Her Tongue

The trauma in my childhood held such a power over me. When I would be walking with my mom, people would always comment, "My, she is such a pretty girl!" After we passed, I would turn around and stick my tongue out at them. The self-hatred was operating in my life. In 1977, I was picked to represent our school in Pennsylvania's annual Flaming Foliage Festival. I didn't really want to go, and couldn't imagine that they would choose me as queen. But,I was picked as runner-up. I was not even excited because I was still wrapped up in shame.

Whenever abuse occurs, a spirit of insanity is present at some level. Abuse normally occurs within a trusted relationship. It is not logical to the person being abused that they would hurt you. Stubbornness and rebellion are often birthed out of abuse or a lack of love. Even when a person is receiving healing from the trauma, it is still very painful to talk about. It is like pulling a splinter out. It hurts to pull it out, but you feel better after it's removed. To leave it in only produces more infection.

"Therefore, since we have this ministry, as we have received mercy, we do not lose heart. But we have renounced the hidden things of shame" (2 Corinthians 4:1–2).

Shame is what the enemy uses to destroy our lives. We need to renounce the hidden things that shame tries to implant into our hearts. Shame makes us think that "Bad things happened to me because I am bad. I have done bad things in my life and this is my punishment." Shame is an emotion, but it is also a deceiving spirit that needs to be renounced. Before Adam and Eve sinned they felt no shame. But as soon as they sinned, shame entered their thoughts. Sin always brings shame. Abuse is sin that is committed against others, and shame is left on the victim as well as the abuser. Many addictive lifestyles of abusers and victims are attempts to remove or obtain temporary reprieve from that shame.

"For the Scripture says, 'Whoever believes on Him will not be put to shame'" (Romans 10:11).

As we believe the Lord's love for us and what He says about us, shame cannot destroy us. When we are abused, things are said or implied through their actions that we start to believe about ourselves. Many Christians struggle receiving the truth that God loves them — not because of unbelief, but because shame has told them that they are unlovable. They feel that no one would love them if they knew what happened to them or what they did. What a lie from the enemy.

"Looking unto Jesus, the author and finisher of our faith, who for the joy that was set before Him endured the cross, despising the shame, and has sat down at the right hand of the throne of God" (Hebrews 12:2).

We were the joy that was set before Jesus. He endured the cross, and was put to open shame for us. He not only carried our sins, but also our shame. Shame is a result of what we have done or what others have done to us. God does not use abuse to punish us. He took our sins as well as our shame on the cross. "Do not fear, for you will not be ashamed; neither be disgraced, for you will not be put to shame; for you will forget the shame of your youth, and will not remember the reproach of your widowhood anymore" (Isaiah 54:4).

Candy, A Lie, And Abandonment Again

While writing this book, I realized that this abuse occurred at the same time of year that John left me. I now understand how these events were so connected in nature and time. I was surprised when I realized that the enemy used the same tools in the divorce as he did at the apple tree. Candy, a lie, and abandonment were part of both events. The enemy is strategic in his attempts to destroy us. During this same time of year, Dale gave me my engagement ring. God wants to enter the cycles of your life that the enemy has established and break out a blessing to move you forward. God is awesome!

This was the most difficult story for me to write. Each of us has certain places that we don't want to even think about, much less to deal with it. The Lord gave me a prophetic word, a dream, and a picture within a week. If it had not been for Dale, this story would not be in this book. He said that this event contained all the key elements of the battle of my life: I was lied to, abused, and then abandoned under that apple tree. I didn't know how to get home. For many years, I was afraid of both being left alone and not knowing where I was.

Laying Down A Relationship

During this period, I started a ministry called "Daughters of Zion." I ministered to many women who had been through abuse and divorce. The Lord used me to help bring deliverance and healing to many broken women. My life was a demonstration of overcoming abuse. Through that ministry I saw marriages restored, which amazed me, as my own had been destroyed. There was emotional healing, too. I saw one

woman come out of a mental institution and a lesbian life-
style and go on to write a book about her own story of deliverance. I also taught women the importance of living a life
of purity.

During this time I had met a guy at a conference in
Canada. We became good friends. Our ministry gifts flowed
well together. We worked together at several conferences in
Canada. I became very fond of him and we started to date.
Some people had prophesied to me that he was the man I
would marry. We started to get serious about our relationship. I told him that I wanted us to go on a three-day fast.
During those three days we wouldn't talk, in order to keep
each from influencing the other. I needed to know if he was
supposed to be my husband, regardless of what the prophets
said. When we first started dating, I felt a "check" deep in
my spirit that he was not my husband, but I didn't want to
accept it. I was tired of being alone.

I was lying on the carpet crying out to God for the
answer when the phone rang. It was a close friend who was
a prophet. I shared with him what I was fasting about. After
praying with me, he said he felt that this man was supposed
to be my husband. After I hung up the phone, something
didn't "sit right" in my spirit. I knew the answer before the
phone call: it was coming out of my spirit, but I didn't want
to hear it. I didn't want to be alone again. However, I knew
that I shouldn't do anything that wasn't God's will. The Lord
answered me with a scripture verse, Ezekiel 14:4. When I
read it, I started to cry. Essentially it states if you go to a
prophet with an idol in your heart, you will hear what you
want to hear. I repented for idolatry and for "going ahead" of
God. I broke the emotional soul tie, the spiritual connection
that grows through relationships, which can keep you tied
to a person and hinder you from moving forward in life. I
picked up the phone and called this man. He was surprised
I called him on the second day of the fast. I knew I needed

to break up with him. I also knew that if I didn't do it then, I would never do it. I told him, "God spoke to me that you are not my husband. I'm asking you not to call me anymore. I need to end the relationship before it goes any further." I was kind of mad at God—I was tired of waiting. Afterward, I had to repent for being angry at Him. The hardest part was going back to church and having so many people ask me why I broke the relationship off. I told them I had to obey God.

I was fighting so many different emotions. My friends Kathy and Mark decided to take me to see Leif Hetland, a prophetic healing evangelist, in Windham, New York. Leif called me up out of the crowd. This is what he prophesied to me: "No more defeat. It's victory time. You will go deeper. You are like Joseph. His own family put him in the pit. You are coming out of the pit and into your destiny. God was testing you. He is testing you in every area. He is teaching you to test the prophetic. You have destiny. That's why it's been so hard for you. I release destiny to come forth for you." That was August 12, 2005.

"What Are You Doing In New York?"

A couple months later, a friend invited me to go see Leif Hetland again in West Chester, Pennsylvania. I wasn't sure where the church was located. But, I'd heard that a pastor I'd previously met at a conference in Toronto, Pastor Tony from Wilmington, Delaware, was also planning on attending this upcoming meeting. I called Pastor Tony and asked him where this church in Pennsylvania was located. He said, "LuAnne, if you are going to West Chester, can you also come out to my church? It's called "the Blessing Place." The two cities were only a short drive from each other.

So, I visited the Blessing Place. During the service, a prophet called me out and told me the following: "Your husband is in Delaware, and God is going to touch your oldest son." Afterward, I drove to Pennsylvania too see Leif Hetland speak. As I walked into the meeting, Leif Hetland said to me, "LuAnne, what are you doing in New York? You don't belong there. God took you to the barren land to make you the King's daughter. You will come back doubly restored." I never saw the connection between those two prophetic words until I wrote this book. I thought I might be going back to Pennsylvania. I was scared because I knew it was the prophetic word from God.

March Forth

I had attended Mt. Zion for eight years. It was the church where I had been set free and taught the truth of God's Word. I thought I would always be there. One night God spoke to me in a dream. He said, "LuAnne, it's time for you to march forth into what I have for you." Then, I left the church, locked the door, and put the key in my purse. As I walked toward my car, Pastor Sweet, who was a staff pastor and a prophet at the church, approached me. He was wearing a long trench coat, "Dick Tracy" style. He asked me why I was leaving. I told him that God had told me it was time to "march forth" and do the things He had for me." Then I woke up from the dream.

I realized we were at the end of February and March was starting in that same week. I wondered if the fourth was a prophetic date, so I checked the calendar. Sunday's date was March 4, 2007. I was blown away that God had spoken to me in such detail. I was thrilled, yet fearful of the unknown. I was also excited! Where I was going? What I was to do? I had to trust God. There were people close to me who didn't understand. I didn't understand it either, but I knew it was God. I had to trust and obey the Lord. I was more afraid of not obeying Him than I was of facing the unknown. If you understand all the details, faith is not required.

God spoke to me. "I want you to go to this church in Rome, New York, and give your testimony. You will be there for just a short time." I remember going to that church and sitting there all by myself. I didn't understand why God had sent me there, but I was obeying the Lord. Pastors Ned and Sue asked me if they could take me to lunch; while there, I shared my testimony with them. Then they asked me if I would share my testimony at their women's meeting that month. I answered, "Yes, God already spoke to me about sharing my testimony in your church." That women's meeting was very powerful.

Matthew, me and Michael in
Stephanie's wedding.

Carleen, Kelly, me and Tina
eating a Symeon's Restaurant.

Chapter 7

DEL-A-WHERE?

I had another dream that would launch me into my destiny. It required an incredible amount of faith. God spoke to me and said, "I want you to move to Delaware." I woke up and exclaimed, "DEL-A-WHERE? God, why do you want me to go to Delaware?" I had such a hard time sleeping that night because I felt such a heavy presence of the Lord on me. As I got up, the Lord said to me, "I want you to look under your bed. There's a book there." I had a stack of pictures of my children, and half-buried beneath them was a book that I had bought for Matthew when he was in second grade. It was the story of Jonah. God said, "Do you want to be like Jonah and not obey Me?" I responded, "God, I will go. I will obey you."

I told Matthew about my dream. He actually got mad at me, and said "Mom, it's not God. God wouldn't take my mother away after Satan took my dad away. "Matthew," I explained, "I know it's God and I need to go. I have to obey Him. I don't understand, but I know He will provide for our every need. I believe this separation will cause you to mature. Even though it seems hurtful now, I believe it will bring forth your destiny."

My friends Dan and Kathy gave me a going-away party at their house. My friends, my son Michael, and some of the pastors from Mt. Zion attended. It was such a blessing. The church in Lowleville also had a sending-off party for me. Pastor Bill took up an offering and gave me $500. The pastor's wife, Rita, prayed for me and said, "This will be for a short season. What you are going for is not what God has for you. It's so much bigger." She knew that God was using the first assignment to connect me to my destiny. I had no idea what God was planning—I just knew I had to obey Him.

The day before I left, I sold my bedroom furniture for $2000. This was all the money that I had to go to Delaware. Pastor Tony from the Blessing Place, had called me a few weeks prior and had asked me to help pastor his church. He told me that God had showed him I was coming to help him, and that he was to ordain me as his assistant pastor. I laughed when he said God had told him to ordain me. He said, "Yes, LuAnne, God told me to ordain you as my assistant pastor."

Where Am I Going To Live?

I left New York on, July 1, 2007. I didn't understand it, but knew I had to obey God. I felt as if I had finally managed to rebuild a life for myself in New York, and now I was giving it all up to move to Delaware. I shut down the cleaning business, my only source of income. All I had was my Jeep and my clothes. I kept asking God "Why?" Why did I have to lay it all back down and trust God for everything again? My son moved into a smaller apartment in the same complex where we had lived. I gave him all my usable possesions for his apartment. I packed my Jeep with some clothes and I left for Delaware. Yes, I was scared. On the way there, I asked the Lord, "Where am I going to stay?" He said, "I will tell you when you get there."

The Blessing Place was located in Wilmington, Delaware, a six-hour drive away. I went inside the church, and Pastor Tony was waiting for me. He smiled and said, "Welcome to the Blessing Place." I went to the restroom before we started talking. While I was in there, tears started streaming down my face. I cried, "God, where I am going live?" The Lord responded," I want you to live in the church." What? Live in the church? After I came out, Pastor Tony said to me, "LuAnne, there is a room upstairs. I believe God wants you to live in the church." I laughed and replied, "Yes, God just spoke that to me in the restroom."

The Blessing Place was a storefront church in Wilmington, Delaware. The church was located near the business district, but we were well acquainted with poverty and neediness. Pastor Tony and Apostle Spady, who was a minister in Delaware for many years, ordained me as Assistant Pastor on June 14, 2007. We ministered to prostitutes, drug addicts, the homeless, inner-city children, and Muslims. God wanted me to know how it felt to be homeless so I could minister to them. The church was open every day. During the summer months, we fed the children daily, and we prayed for people every day. Many people came in off the streets and gave their lives to Christ. There were many miracles with healings and deliverances.

The church met on the first floor, and I lived on the second floor. I slept on an air mattress for two months. I don't think God let me go home to get my day bed for those first two months because He knew I wouldn't have come back. It wasn't easy. I had to bathe using a small sink and a washcloth. One day I was shaving my legs, and had rested one foot on the sink, which suddenly fell off the wall. Water went everywhere! I declared, "In the name of Jesus, Satan, you're not having my sink!" I picked the sink off the floor, put it back on the wall, reconnected the PVC plumbing, and finished the job! The enemy tried to discourage me, but I laughed and moved on. I showered once a week at my niece's house an hour away. She nicknamed me "Aunt Jesus."

The ministry at the Blessing Place was very exciting. You never knew who would walk through the door and what their needs would be. One day a woman walked into the church with her thirty-year-old daughter. Her daughter had gangrene and the doctor wanted to remove her toes. The mother asked if I would please pray for her. I took a bottle of anointing oil, poured oil over the daughter's toes, and prayed, "In the name of Jesus Christ, I break the power of witchcraft that has been done over you, and I command them to be healed in the name of Jesus." The daughter told me she had just delivered twins. Her one son was in Philadelphia Children's Hospital and was not expected to live. She asked if I could please pray for her baby. I prayed in the name of Jesus and I bound the spirit of death and commanded it to release that baby boy. Then I commanded life into him and declared that he would be healed and made whole.

The daughter came back the next day to tell me how the Lord had healed her toes. The natural color had returned to them again. She also said her son was doing much better in the hospital. He was released a few days later. God had given her two miracles. It was awesome to see all the miracles God did at the Blessing Place.

You Are Like Jacob

It was September 7, 2007. I was downstairs in the church worshiping to the song "Let It Rain." I was alone, and was crying out to God. "God, why did you send me here? Lord, I need a breakthrough in my life! Speak to me. Why am I in Delaware? I feel like Jacob! God, I'm not letting You go until You bless me!" I heard someone knocking at the door. Two women from the church asked me if I would take them to Destiny Church in Dover, Delaware, to see Prophet Sharon

Stone. They told me it was Pastor Dale Mast's church. I commented, "Sure, I'd love to see Sharon Stone, but who is Dale Mast?" They told me he was an awesome prophet in Dover.

As we walked into the church I said to them, "I wish we had a church like this." As I walking down the aisle to get a seat, a man took the microphone and started to prophesy. He proclaimed,"There are people here like Jacob that are crying out to God, 'I am not letting you go until you bless me!'" One of the women I was with turned to me and said, "Pastor LuAnne, you said that to the Lord right before we left. Every time we go somewhere, God always gives you a word!"

After the service, I walked up to Pastor Dale and told him what I had prayed before coming to his church that very night. "It was the very same words that you spoke tonight when I came through the door. I was crying out to God, asking him, 'Why did he send me to Delaware?'" Pastor Dale responded, "Raise your right hand." He put his right hand up to my right hand and said, "I am in agreement with you that you are not going to let go of God until He blesses you." It was a very powerful prophetic declaration that he spoke over me.

On November 4, 2007, I went to the "Voice of the Apostles Conference" at Life Center, a church in Harrisburg, Pennsylvania. I was worshiping at the front of the church, praying for my sons and asking God to bring them godly wives. A young woman who had been worshiping in dance on the stage came down and started prophesying over me. She said, "Don't give up on praying for your sons. God is going to bring them godly wives. The Lord is also getting ready to release your husband. God has an awesome call on your life." I thought, "Release my husband? Where is he? Is he in prison?" I couldn't understand what it meant. Later, I understood its meaning, even though it was very unusual. Dale, who is now my husband, was married at that time. Fourteen days after I received that prophetic word, Dale's wife went to be with the Lord after a two-year battle with cancer.

On November 15, Prophet Russell Hill came to the Blessing Place for the first time. He started to prophesy over me: "You are a prophetess. You have given up much. In the last seven years, all that has been taken from you, the Lord says, 'It is all coming back.' I see a house and a new car for you. Everything that was taken will be brought back. I see you on TBN. 'You will be on TV,' says the Lord. You are going to be very wealthy. You're like Esther with a scepter." Living in a storefront church, that promise seemed distant. Yet, I knew God was moving because of all the prophetic words I kept receiving from numerous people at different meetings.

Taken To Another Place

The next day I returned to the Blessing Place from my niece's house. As I was walking to my room the Lord said, "I want you to open your Bible, lie down on the bed, and read the Word." As soon as I opened my Bible, I fell into a deep sleep and then into a dream.

In the dream I was listening to Randy Clark teaching about people who had experienced a supernatural encounter of leaving their body and going to heaven. He said that he had 0had an encounter of being taken up, but when he got to the ceiling he couldn't go through it. He kept experiencing fear, which stopped him from passing through. I said, "God take me. I want to visit heaven." At that second, it felt like a vacuum cleaner sucked my spirit out of my body and I was looking down at my body on the daybed. I started traveling up and out of the building and into space. It felt like I was an airplane going about 20,000 miles an hour. I was traveling so fast, and it started getting darker and darker. I pleaded with the Lord, "Please don't take me to hell. I don't want to see hell. Take me to heaven. I want to see heaven." I came to a sudden stop, and I was standing on the earth looking at this large field. It was full of army tanks and trucks. I asked the Lord, "Why am I seeing this?" The next thing I knew, I was traveling through the air again. I came back down into my body and I woke up. I asked, "Lord, why did you take me there? Why did you show me this?" He replied, "I'm getting ready to unleash My army on the devil for what he has done to My people." I called Pastor Tony and I shared my experience. Then I called Rick Sodmont, who'd also had similar experiences. I explained to him what just happened to me. He assured me, "LuAnne, I know that it's God, because that describes the same kind of out-of-body experiences I have had.

Giving Diamonds

During our December conference at the Blessing Place, Prophet Joe Mercer and his wife, Doleen, came from Tampa, Florida, to preach. While Doleen was preaching, the Lord spoke to me: "I want you to give Doleen your diamond tennis bracelet." I started arguing with the Lord: "Not my bracelet!" He replied, "If you give it to her, I will break poverty off of you." I couldn't get that bracelet off fast enough! I stood up while she was preaching and said, "The Lord asked me to bless you with this bracelet." She started crying with excitement because she had always wanted one. Little did I know that what God had promised was closer than I could have ever imagined.

I drove back home to New York for Christmas; I was very excited to see my sons. It was hard for them to cope with my living in Delaware. They couldn't understand how or why I would live in a church in Delaware. The area I lived in could be dangerous at times, and this worried them. Someone had been murdered one block away from the church, and as with many inner city areas, drugs and alcohol were a major part of the night life.

It was a hard Christmas for me. It was great to be with my sons, but they were angry with me for my decision. They yelled at me and told me I was crazy and needed to move back to New York. I knew they were afraid for me and concerned about where my life was going. But, I knew I was in the Lord's will, so I had no fear. During my time at the Blessing Place, God supernaturally protected me and met all my financial needs. I received no income, but when a bill was due, God would always send someone to give me what I needed. I went to a house church meeting in Maryland to hear John Scotland, an evangelist, speak. After he was done ministering to the people, he came over to the couch where I was sitting and pulled out his wallet. He said that God had told him to give me a specific amount of money so that I could make my car payment. It was exactly what I needed! He also told me that my season at the Blessing Place was over, and that God was getting ready to open a new door for me, and it was going to more than I could ever ask for. Every bill was paid on time even though I received no income from the Blessing Place. We ministered almost every day, from ten in the morning until ten at night. I had some Mondays off. I knew I was in God's will, though many people close to me didn't understand.

As I was driving back to Delaware, it became clear to me that my life as I knew it before in New York was over. I was excited to get back to Delaware. We were having a New Year's Eve conference at the church, and the speaker was Abner Suarez, a prophet from Dunn, North Carolina. God told him not to leave the church until he met the assistant pastor. I came back a day later. Abner was concerned about the lack of unity in the church leadership. That lack of unity became the starting point for my transition out of the Blessing Place and into my future. Sometimes God will not allow certain things to work out so that He can move you into your future.

A Man of Excellence

I preached that Sunday morning at the Blessing Place; I gave my testimony and prayed for people. Pastor Cooper, who shared the building with us on some Sundays, started to prophesy over a man whom I had become good friends with who had come to hear me preach. Pastor Cooper said, "You are a man of greatness." I was standing behind my friend as he received this word. As I heard it, I literally stepped back from him as I remembered a prophetic word that a minister from Brazil had given me years earlier. Rapha had prophesied, "You are an awesome woman of God ... You are not going to marry a man of 'greatness,' but a man of 'excellence,' says the Lord." At that second, I knew this man of "greatness" was not the husband God had for me.

Then Pastor Cooper prayed for me. He said, "I believe that God is getting ready to open a door for you for ministry. You are very anointed. Marriage is coming soon. Are you ready to be married?" He asked me this question three times! Yes, I was, but where was he? Where was this man of excellence?

It's Time To Leave Again

The same day I met Abner, my friends Mark and Kathy stopped in to visit. God had told them to come check up on me. A few days after they left, another friend flew out from Seattle to see me. God was speaking to my friends about my situation. Apparently while I was in New York for Christmas, someone had driven a wedge between the pastor and me by the things that they said. It affected my relationship with the pastor, which didn't recover until after I had left the church.

During this time, the Lord led me to Zephaniah 3:18–20. The verses are as follows:

"The LORD has promised: Your sorrow has ended, and you can celebrate. I will punish those who mistreat you. I will bring together the lame and the outcasts, then they will be praised, instead of despised, in every country on earth. I will lead you home, and with your own eyes you will see me bless you with all you once owned. Then you will be famous everywhere on this earth. I, the LORD, have spoken!" (Contemporary English Version)

God will always use His Word to speak to us. His Word is powerful.

During a time of worship and prayer, I pleaded, "Lord, what about the bills this month?" I heard Him say to me: "Let go and let God. A wedding is coming for you. Be prepared to be married soon. The dress, the shoes, and the honeymoon. What is your desire?" I always wanted my prince to sweep me off my feet on a white horse. My dream was to go to Hawaii on a honeymoon.

Shortly thereafter, four prophets came to the Blessing Place at different times, and each prophesied to me that a change was coming: "The house, the car, and the husband are nothing for God." "You're going to need the car for what God has for you." "Get ready! God is about to blow you away. Don't you dare to give up now. You are about to break through." The fourth prophet said, "The Lord said you have been faithful with little, now God is going bless you with much. You are about to be spiritually promoted." They all gave variations of the same word. I was excited, but I couldn't understand how God was going to break through this hard place. But, I knew he would. During a meeting at the Blessing Place, Karen, a personal friend, gave me this word: "You have given it all up for the Lord. No one gives up houses and family that God does not reward. The Lord is *so* going to bless you. I hear the Lord say, 'The blessings will overtake you.'"

God gave me a dream soon after. In the dream there was a yellow mantle across the back of my shoulders. As I was walking out of the Blessing Place, I laid the mantle on a chair, grabbed my suitcases, and walked out the door. I woke up from the dream and asked God, "What does this dream mean?" He answered, "It's time for you to leave the Blessing Place." I retorted, 'Lord, what?" He reiterated, "It's time for you to leave." "Lord, if it's time for me to leave, confirm it for me." The phone rang. Pastor Rose from New York, who had given me my first prophetic word, called me with another: "God told me to tell you to get out now! Don't wait another day!" I knew God was serious about me moving forward into my future.

The Lord indicated that I needed to pack up my things and write up my resignation. He said that at that evening's board meeting the pastor would bring up five issues, and then I was to hand him my resignation. I wrote the letter and packed up all of my things that afternoon. At the beginning of the meeting, the pastor stood up and raised several issues, just like the Lord said he would. They were very small things that weren't even important. I started counting on my hand under the table. When he finished with the fourth one, he stopped. I thought I had missed it. Then he started again. When he finished the fifth one, God urged, "Give him your resignation now."

I stood up and gave him my resignation. I told him, "God told me you were going to bring up five issues, and when you did, I was to hand you my resignation. As of January 27, 2008, I am no longer the assistant pastor of the Blessing Place. Here is my resignation." Pastor Tony dropped his head; I walked out of the meeting. The next morning I met him at the church to return my key. He didn't want me to leave; he felt leaving wasn't God's will for me. But the Lord had showed me that it was time to go. I know all of this happened to move me into what God had for me, and to also help me overcome my fear of authority. Looking back, I realized if I hadn't obeyed God and left when I did, I would have missed Dale preaching at Destiny Church that next Sunday. It was his last Sunday before leaving on a two-week mission trip to Burma.

It was a very important victory for me, as well as a crucial step in establishing God's plan for my life. I could never stand up for myself in front of spiritual authority. Doing so broke the patterns of abuse that started in my childhood and extended into my Christian walk. I walked out of the Blessing Place not knowing where I was going. After I got into my Jeep, I started to cry. I questioned God: "What did I just do? Did I do the right thing by giving up everything in New York to move here? Maybe they were right. Maybe I missed it."

"By faith Abraham, when he was called, obeyed and went forth to a place which he was destined to receive as an inheritance; and he went, although he did not know or trouble his mind about where he was to go" (Hebrews 11:8, Amplified Bible).

My going away party in New York to move to Delaware.

More friends at the going away party.

My sending off and offering blessing from the
Lowville Church.

I was praying for a young girl at The Blessing
Place who fell under the power of the Spirit.

Hakeem, me and Naim. They prophesied that "the
house, the car and the husband is nothing for God."

Abner, a minister I met at the Blessing Place, who
spoke into my future.

Chapter 8

Fear Of The Unknown

I was fighting my doubts and fears because of past disappointments and hurts. It felt like I was being evicted from my home all over again. I lamented, "God, I gave up everything to come and serve You." I felt Him say, "Your serving wasn't in vain. It's time to go forward." I recalled how God had provided in the past, and I knew He would do it again: I just had to trust Him. I realized my fear was just the enemy trying to gain ground in my mind. The objections of all the people who had told me I was nuts to leave my church, my business, and my family kept going through my mind. Fear was trying to keep me from entering into my future blessings. I cried out to God, "Now what, God? Where do I go?"

At that moment the phone rang. It was Carol, a friend I had met at the Blessing Place. "LuAnne," she said, "God told me you are not to leave Delaware. God is not done with you here." She invited me to stay with her in her apartment until God revealed what I was to do next. After unpacking my things in her spare bedroom, I asked her, "Where do you want to go to church this weekend?" She mentioned going to Life Center in Harrisburg, Pennsylvania. I said, "Let's pray and see what God shows us." As I walked into my bedroom,

the Lord spoke to me: "I want you to go to Dover Destiny."
"Dover Destiny!" I said, "Why Dover Destiny?"

I told Carol what God had shown me. She said God
mentioned the same thing to her. So that Sunday we drove
to Destiny Church where Dale Mast was the pastor. As I
walked inside it brought back the memories of the meeting in
September when I visited to hear Sharon Stone. "God, why
did you send me here?" After worship ended, Pastor Dale
prophesied over Carol, then preached his sermon. I thought
he was an awesome teacher and I enjoyed his preaching. I
prayed, "Lord, I am not leaving here until You give me a
word. I need a word from You. Why am I at Dover Destiny?
Is this my church?" The service ended, and I didn't get a
word from God during the service. Pastor Dale announced
they had prophetic teams available who would prophesy
over you after the service, and if you wanted to receive a
prophetic word, please go to the right side of the church.
I went over and I sat in the chair and I waited and waited.
Nobody from the prophetic team showed up. Pastor Dale
told me this was the first time that this had ever happened.

Two people came up to me to tell me they would go find
somebody and send them right over. I waited for fifteen minutes, but no one came. That Sunday, Pastor Dale had prophesied for those who had a birthday in February. He had just
finished praying with the last person. "God, I'm not leaving
here until I get a word from you. I guess I'll have to go to
the 'big guy.'" I walked over to Pastor Dale and asked him
to pray for me. "I need a word from God."

His prophecy spoke to my situation, and addressed some
of the difficulties I had gone through. Among other things,
he prophesied, "You are in a narrow hallway. God is taking
you through something to take you to something."

He continued, "You know God never shuts a door
without opening up another, but there can be a little pause
in the hallway. It's that pearl that comes out of the situation.

What's your name?" I responded, "LuAnne." He resumed, "LuAnne, I want you to take my hand. Lord, as I take her hand, I take it in the fellowship of the Spirit. You need to know that you are being received here. I break off everything that has made you feel rejected or abandoned, or where your voice was not heard, or where your intentions were questioned. I break off the bitterness of your soul, and I speak a release of the love and favor of God. I heard the Lord say, 'O Daughter of Zion, ascend, and don't let go of the vision.' There were times when Jacob had to separate from Esau to literally allow the dream to go forward. The Lord says, 'There is a time that you will grow, with a time of separation, with wisdom of my spirit.' God says, 'I am never shoving you out of my plan, I am always shoving you in.' God says, 'You see in part and prophecy in part, but I am helping you to walk through and get to your place of fruitfulness.' God says, 'Watch how I start to move through your life in a new way. There is coming a new glory on you. You are going to rest in a place of fellowship that is going to empower you into your next season, O Daughter of Zion. The place the enemy broke up, I am going to start watering.' That place seems like a desert, and God says, 'That's the place that I'm going to start to water.'"

After Dale was done ministering to me, I mentioned that it was my son Michael's birthday that day. He asked me, "How old is your son?" I wondered why he was asking me that. At a later point, he told me he couldn't guess my age and that he was interested in me. When he learned my son was older than his, he said I was "fair game."

I felt that God wanted me to attend this church, but I didn't understand why. I knew God was prompting me to go there. After we left, I asked Carol if we could drive down to the beach. I said, "Carol, I need to get alone with God. I want to ask Him a question." As I walked along the beach, I began praying. I intended to ask the Lord, "Why did You send me to Dover Destiny?" But, much to my surprise, the first thing I blurted out was, "Is Dale my husband? Lord, is that why You sent me to Destiny?" I didn't hear God say anything. I didn't share this with anyone until later.

The next day Pastor Dale was going to Burma. The Lord had given me a burden to pray and intercede for him. The "burden" wouldn't lift. I would even wake up in the middle of the night and pray for him. He shared with me later that the Christians were being greatly persecuted in Burma, and some were even being martyred in remote jungle areas.

The next Sunday, Carol and I went back to church at Destiny. Dale was still in Burma. As I walked up to the door, I reached for the handle and heard the Lord say, "You're going to be the 'First Lady' here." I laughed to myself— the First Lady? After the service I went to the Hallmark to buy Matthew a birthday card. I was standing at the register to pay for the card when a woman interrupted us and asked the sales woman, "Do you have any First Lady cards here?" Internally, I laughed again, because I knew God was speaking to me again to confirm it.

The following week I went up to New York to visit my sons. It was Matthew's birthday. He was very excited to tell me that he had just "met someone," a young woman named Nichole. Also, God had just given him a promotion at work. He became a department manager at the very young age of twenty-three. I knew God was breaking through in his life. I said, "Matthew, I knew God would come through. He has been so faithful. I am so proud of you. I believe that's why God took me out of your life, so God could open you up to your future." I had a great week in New York with them.

"Take Care Of Dale"

Driving back to Delaware, I was looking forward to seeing what God had for me at Destiny. The Lord didn't speak to me that day, but I had a dream that night. In the dream, a woman I didn't know spoke to me: "LuAnne, take care of Dale and continue the vision for revival at Destiny." I woke up shaking. Who was that woman who visited me in a dream? I looked at the clock—it was 5:55 in the morning. Somehow I knew that specific time had a prophetic meaning, and I asked God what it meant. He said to me, "Apostolic." I also knew that *five* meant "grace." I heard, "Grace, grace, grace" in my spirit.

I went to my computer and opened up Destiny's website. The woman in my dream was Dale's deceased wife. Even though she had passed away months ago, her picture was still on the website. I started shaking again. "God, what are you saying? Is this why You sent me to Delaware? Is Dale my husband? Lord, if this is true, I need You to confirm it." Then I remembered a prophecy that Prophet Joe Mercer had given me the first time I visited the Blessing Place: "LuAnne, your husband is in Delaware."

Look What I Got For Twenty Bucks!

The next time I visited Destiny, Pastor Dale asked me if I wanted to minister with Destiny's prophetic team at a church in Norristown, Pennsylvania. I said I'd love to go. Pastor Dale preached at that church, and I was so blessed by the teaching and the prophetic mantle on his life. Before the church took the offering, he said, "In the Old Testament, the scriptures tell us that when [the Israelites] would bring their offerings, God would meet them. As you give your offering tonight, tell God what you want. Don't just ask God to bless you, tell Him specifically what you want."

I prayed, "All I have is $20. I know it is not much, Lord, but it is all the money I have left." I put that $20 bill into the offering and I told God, "You spoke to me in a dream that Dale was my husband and now I am asking—I want Dale for my husband." Later, Dale told me that he realized that night that he was being drawn toward me. He stood behind the pulpit in a position so that the person in the front row would block my face so he could concentrate on his sermon. I didn't know at that time that Dale was also interested in me. He told me weeks later that he knew he was falling in love with me that night.

Carol and Nina. Carol called me and said, "God
is not done with you in Delaware."

Chapter 9

He Makes All Things New

D ale asked me to come to the church to talk to me about my past ministry experiences and what my vision was for my future. I shared with him about my deliverance anointing and the call on my life to minister to the abused. I told him about having gone on three international trips with Randy Clark and Global Awakening. We talked and shared for over four hours. I asked Dale if he knew Randy. Dale said he had taught at Global Awakening's ministry school, Global School of Supernatural Ministry, for two years, but hadn't met Randy. I informed him Carol and I were going to hear Randy speak that Sunday night. Dale wanted to go, and said he'd pick us up at five that evening.

Five minutes before Dale was supposed to arrive, Carol decided that she didn't want to go. So it ended up that just Dale and I went. Two months earlier a friend named Leslie told me a dream she had about me. "LuAnne," Leslie said, "I saw you with this man and you're so happy. You left the Blessing Place and Pastor Tony was sad. I believe this man you were with is the husband God has for you." In the dream, she saw me driving up to a church where Pastor Tony was standing outside, and I entered the church with this man.

As we drove into the church's parking lot, Leslie's dream started coming back to me.

Dale dropped me off and went to park the car. I saw Pastor Tony standing outside of the church talking on his phone. He had received a call during the worship service and had come out to pray for the caller. I was walking toward the church. Our paths crossed, and Pastor Tony asked me when I was coming back. I told him I wasn't coming back, and that I was going to Dale Mast's Church. He said, "Pastor Dale Mast?" The church door opened, and Leslie herself walked out of the church. She also had received a phone call—her mom was lost and needed directions. Leslie looked at me as Dale walked up. She started smiling and said, "Oh my gosh! The dream I had about you is unfolding right before my eyes!"

As we walked into the church, the worship team was singing the song "He Makes All Things New." The church was very crowded, and Dale was looking for seats as I went up to talk to Randy Clark. Many of the people from the Blessing Place were there and were very happy to see me. Several people ran up to me and hugged me. I walked over to Randy Clark and asked him, "Do you know who Dale Mast is?" He said, "Yes, I do." I said, "Dale wants to meet you." He said, "Bring him up here." So, I brought Dale up to meet Randy.

As we were walking toward Randy, the worship leader called out Dale's name. He said, "Pastor Dale, six years ago you prophesied to me that I would be a worship leader who would open the heavens and prophesy over people. You prophesied over me then. Now I am prophesying over you: 'What the enemy meant for evil, God is about to turn it around for your good. God is about to make all things new.'" He prophesied other words that were a blessing as well.

As this worship leader was prophesying, Randy Clark had his arm around Dale on one side. I was standing on the other side in front of Dale. I leaned my head back onto him. Randy and I were both praying for Dale as this worship leader continued to prophesied over him. After the worship leader finished prophesying, I introduced Dale to Randy. It was quite a night! We knew that the prophecy which spoke of "all things new" had to do with our relationship and our ministry.

As the praise and worship continued, Pastor Tony came up front to worship. I went over to him and said, "Pastor Tony, I don't want anything between us. I thank God for you." The presence of God was so great that we both fell on the floor as everyone was worshipping at the front of the church. The wall between us came crashing down.

Our First Kiss

That night, I knew there was something special about our relationship. Dale drove me back to the apartment, and parked in front of the door. We talked until three in the morning. When we said goodbye, Dale just sat in the car and watched me walk to the front door. He told me later that he wanted to walk me to the door, but he couldn't figure out how to say goodbye. A handshake would be impersonal, but a hug could be too close to a kiss, so he just sat in the car! He felt it was a "safe option." Dale asked if I would be interested in going out to Life Center (a three-hour drive away) on Wednesday evening to hear Apostle Che Ahn (whose ministry is based in California) speak. I told him I would enjoy the opportunity.

Tuesday night I went to the weekly intercessory prayer meeting at Destiny. When I came into the church that night, the thought suddenly occurred to one of the church's leaders that I would make a good wife for Pastor Dale. Angie, who led intercession, had a dream that night. In her dream, I was talking to Pastor Dale, but kept calling him "Dale." She said,

"You don't know him that well. He is Pastor Dale to you." To which I replied, "No, we are more than that."

After I got home from the prayer meeting that night, I had a hard time sleeping. I was so excited about being with Dale. God had showed me that Dale was going to be my husband. I got up around two o'clock, early Wednesday morning. I knew I had to put my thoughts on paper or I wouldn't be able to get to sleep. I wrote him an email telling him how I felt. But after I finished writing, God told me not to send it, but to print it out and give it to Dale the next day. I put the letter into my purse, waiting for the right time to give it to him.

Dale picked me up early that morning so that we could spend some extra time in the Lancaster area before the meeting that night. As he opened the car door for me, he commented that he couldn't sleep last night. He asked me how I slept. I didn't dare tell him. After driving for an hour, we stopped to get some coffee. My mind was racing with thoughts and feelings for him. I felt as if I would explode, but I was also battling the fear of disappointment. God had made me wait for seven years, turn down relationships, move from New York, leave my children and friends, and close my business to go live in a church. Was this the reason why God had me do all of that? Was it really going to happen for me? Is this what all those prophecies were about? Dale came around and opened my door, and we walked inside to order our coffees. As we were in line, I felt such a peace come over me about the relationship. I didn't know when to give him the letter, but halfway through the line to order, that fear lifted and was replaced by a sense of peace. We both ordered French Vanilla coffee and headed back to the car. (Just now as I was writing this, we both started laughing because we are drinking French Vanilla coffee!) After we got back on the road, Dale turned to me and said, "I had a hard time sleeping last night. All I could think about was you. I have feelings for you." I reached into my purse, pulled out the email I'd written him, and said, "You need to read this letter I wrote to you last night. I couldn't sleep either until I wrote my feelings down." Since he was driving, he asked if I would read it to him.

"Dear Dale, I couldn't sleep last night, so I decided to write my feelings down. Ever since I met you, I felt like my heart came alive again. As soon as I met you, it was so easy to talk with you. I feel like you've been my best friend forever. I don't know where this relationship is going, but I do know that I do have feelings for you. But, I trust the Lord that he will lead us from here."

We started holding hands; God was doing a sweet thing in our lives. We stopped to eat lunch at the Warwick Restaurant in Hummellstown, Pennsylvania. When we walked into the restaurant entrance, which is a semi-private long narrow hallway, we both stopped. Dale put his arm around me to give me a hug. I slowly leaned toward him and gently kissed him. It was a very special moment for both of us. He told me later that he had been "stuck," and this broke him free to move forward into our relationship and life.

The very next day, Dale met with Angie and another church leader at the church. He was very anxious to talk with them. The phone rang in the church office and the other leader answered the phone. Dale waited for a minute and then asked if she could call them back later. Angie turned to Dale and asked, "What did you do, run off and get married?" He told them, "Something like that. I know that LuAnne will be my wife" He was so excited and blessed to know that God had brought me into his life. He had prayed and asked God to bring his wife to him. God brought me all the way from New York to "DEL-A-WHERE." After we were married Dale told me it was not "DEL-A-WHERE," but "DALE-AWARE."

We were both excited to see the new thing God was doing in our lives after we had both experienced so much loss and tragedy. God was restoring back to us what the enemy had stolen. It had been a long seven years for me. I wasn't going to marry just anybody! I wanted the one God had for me. I knew Dale was God's will because of the supernatural signs, prophecies, and dreams I'd received, as well as the release of God's perfect timing that allowed us to meet as I obeyed Him.

Dale and I spent a lot of time together during our short courtship and we enjoyed every minute of it. God moved in so many different ways in that special time. God's restoration is better than we could ever imagine or plan.

Eight Red Roses

One morning Dale knocked on the door. I opened it, and he came inside holding eight red roses. He knelt down on one knee in front of me and said, "LuAnne, here are eight red roses. Seven of these roses are for the seven years of hell you went through that are covered by the blood of Jesus. The eighth rose is for 'new beginnings.' Will you marry me?" I said, "I would be honored to be your wife. Yes, I will marry you." He replied, "Get in the car. This is going to be a day you will never forget." I assured him it already had been.

BMW

After we had lunch, we approached the BMW dealership we had visited the day before. Dale had said he'd never really looked at BMWs and he wanted to check them out. I didn't think he showed any real interest in buying one. (He told me later me he was trying to figure out which color I liked; I had no idea what he was up to.)

We turned into the car dealership, and I said, "What are you doing?" He answered, "I bought you a BMW." "Don't you play with me!" I implored. We walked into the dealership, and the salesman handed me keys to a BMW 7 Series. The salesman grinned and said, "Congratulations. It's yours." Dale had shared the story with the salesman, and it really touched him and he enjoyed his part in my miracle. I started crying—I had believed God for this car.

There was an explosion inside of my spirit. I was so excited I wanted to scream! The husband I had believed for and the car! I wanted someone to pinch me to make sure I wasn't dreaming. I knew Dale had bought the car, but I also knew the Lord had kept his promise to me from six years before. When I had no vehicle or money, I laid my hands on that BMW 7 Series in New York and had believed God for it. As Dale was signing the papers, I noticed the salesman's name on his desk: Joe Coverdale. I laughed out loud. "LuAnne," God said, "You are going to 'cover Dale!'" I know Cinderella rode in a pumpkin carriage, but my prince bought me a BMW!

Texting

After we picked up our BMW, we went for a drive. I was so excited about the marriage proposal (and the car, of course). All I had believed the Lord for was coming to pass. I couldn't wait to tell my sons what had just happened to me. So, I did what they do to me all the time—I texted them a message. "I met Dale. He bought me a BMW. We are getting married." They both called me right away! They didn't know I was seeing anyone, much less seriously enough to be getting married. Mike's friend, Rachel, said that he needed to get on his knees and ask my forgiveness for making fun of me and for not believing me. He did exactly that, and he also said, "I know the God you serve is real. I'm so happy for you. You deserve everything you want for what you have gone through. I'm very proud of you." Matt was also very excited. He said, "Mom, God never ceases to amaze me and neither do you." God has been so faithful. When Dale and I tell the story of how God brought us together, we say that BMW stands for "Be My Wife!"

Dale's Dream

We were trying to decide when to get married. We knew timing was important. There were many factors involved that made choosing a date very difficult. One night Dale had a dream. In the dream, we were standing next to each other in a large meeting place. Apostle Chuck Pierce (under whom Dale was ordained) came up to us and greeted us. He turned around and we all skated toward the front of the hall to get married.

We wrote Chuck an email asking him if he could officiate our wedding on June 7, 2008. We knew he seldom performed weddings, but because of the dream we felt we should ask. Chuck responded that unfortunately he was unable to fit our wedding into his schedule. We realized, however, God was showing us that this was the right date for us to be married because of the dream. The date was 6-7-8. This sequence has a very significant prophetic meaning: *six* represents "man," *seven* represents "God," and *eight* represents "a new beginning." God spoke to us even through the numbers of the date of our wedding. We were stepping into God's will for a new beginning! So, we set the date for our wedding on 6.7.08. (Chuck sent us a video-recorded "blessing" that we played at the wedding. We were really touched by it.)

One Shoe Can Change Your Life

A friend from the church threw a surprise "Cinderella-themed" wedding shower for me. I was out with Dale, and he told me he needed to stop and pick something up from the church. When we went inside, I was surprised and greeted by women from the church. They had placed a pumpkin carriage cutout on the stage. They had me sit down in a chair, and had Dale come out with a shoe to put on my foot. It was a great time. My friends in Utica, New York, also threw a wedding shower for me. God even spoke to someone to buy my wedding dress. God provided in so many awesome ways.

We had a lot of fun planning our wedding. We decided to have all of our children in our wedding party: Michael, Benjamin, Heidi, Matthew, Andrew, and Zachary. I chose to walk down the aisle to Brian and Jenn Johnson's song, "Where You Go, I'll Go." This song had great significance for me when I had first heard it a Global Awakening conference in Pennsylvania. While I was living in New York, I listened to it over and over again. I used to play it before I would go to sleep. I told the Lord, "I will go where you go, and I'll say what you say." I realized this song was my life's testimony. I did what God asked me to do. I walked away from everything I had—away from the old and the familiar—and into the unknown. I felt like Ruth in the Bible: she left everything she knew to meet her Boaz. Dale is definitely my Boaz!

My dad walked me partway up the aisle; my sons, standing on either side of me, escorted me the rest of the way. When it was asked, "Who gives this bride in marriage?" my sons responded in unison, "We do!" Later, they said that they were happy and relieved to know that I was going to be well taken care of. I realized then how much fear they had for me being alone. They carried a heavy burden of responsibility for me. They were glad I met Dale. They knew he would take care of me. Michael and Matthew both spoke during the wedding. They said they were happy for me and proud of me. They spoke about my faith and love for God. They shared how I believed God when I was stripped of everything, and how God was restoring it all.

It was awesome to see our children surrounding us during the ceremony. At the end of the wedding, we left the church to the song "He Makes All Things New." That was the song they were singing at the church when Dale and I walked in together to meet Randy Clark. It was our first unofficial, unplanned date. Many of my friends from New York and the Blessing Place attended the wedding. It was great to have our families there as well. Many there had watched me walk through those difficult times, and they rejoiced when they saw what the Lord had done. There were so many miracles surrounding our wedding. We followed our wedding up with a wonderful honeymoon in Hawaii—another dream came true!

Dale was the man of excellence. Every time we get into a disagreement, he reminds me that God Himself stated that he (Dale) was a man of excellence! God has really blessed me with a wonderful husband who cherishes me and my children. When God picks your husband you will never be disappointed.

6-7-8

A year later we were getting ready to celebrate our wedding anniversary. We had to speak in New Jersey before we left for Florida for a vacation. Driving up to New Jersey, we passed three Delaware cars with the numbers "678" in their tag number in that particular order. At the church where we were ministering, we were preceded by a special musical performance. A woman sang a song we had used in our wedding! I recognized it right away. Dale didn't, because it was sung differently. After I brought the song to his attention, we both started laughing. When we arrived in Florida, the room number of the condo where we were staying was "6708." The exact date of our wedding! Every day was a reminder that we were in God's perfect will.

Later, we were registering our vehicle at the DMV. They were offering bicentennial license plates featuring five-digit license plate numbers and only had three left. I asked them if they had one with 678 in it. They did. 77678! The tag was very significant to us. I waited seven years to be married to Dale, and he waited seven months to marry me. The double 7s are God's "double blessing" on our marriage.

Four Rooms, Four Months

Dale's house was on the market with a real estate agent for nine months, but they couldn't sell it. We were ministering in Japan when we saw a real estate sign that read "MAST Real Estate Sales." Our host said it was an acrostic of the owners' names. Dale and I felt it signified we were going to sell that house ourselves.

On our long flight home from Japan, I leaned over to Dale and asked him to pray and give me a prophetic word. He said he was too tired. I insisted, "I need a word from God." So, he grabbed his notebook and started seeking the Lord for a word. He started writing. This is what the Holy Spirit said to him on May 21, 2009: "It is time to pick out the furniture that will fill and fit the house. For I am moving you into your new position for the next season. Four rooms in four months. I am giving you a renewed hope and expectation. The furniture will fit the place. For I am opening up new gates of supply. New leather will speak to you."

We had been looking at houses since we had been married. Several months after we returned from Japan, we were still looking. I started complaining to Dale about the delay in finding our house. He replied, "You didn't do what God asked you to do, so He is waiting for you. You haven't picked out the furniture yet." I said, "What? Who picks out new furniture before they have a house?" I felt a rebuke from the Lord, and remembered the following scripture: "'For My thoughts *are* not your thoughts, nor *are* your ways My ways,' says the Lord" (Isaiah 55:8). "Wow," I thought. "Who am I not to trust God after all He has done for me?" So, I went furniture shopping.

As we walked into the store, a sales associate asked us if we needed any help. We told her we were picking out new furniture for our new house, and she said, "What are the colors of your walls?" I started laughing and responded, "I don't know." She looked puzzled, and I explained. I shared my testimony of losing everything and how God was restoring it all back. She became teary-eyed as I shared my life story. Later, she said she was very blessed by our story. We picked out all new furniture, four rooms of it. I prayed, "Okay God, we have the furniture, now where is our house?"

Dale's house had just come off the market with the real estate agent a few weeks before we bought the furniture. After I did what God instructed, we sold his house that week and bought the beautiful home where we now live. We moved into the house four months after receiving that word from the Lord. God had restored ALL THINGS NEW. The living room outfit was burgundy leather. God had said, "New leather will speak to you."

10.10.10

Our church's youth leader, Maurice Suggs, approached us one Sunday and said that God kept speaking to him about "10.10.10." He felt God was indicating that something awesome was going to happen on that date. Earlier in the year we had invited Bishop Bill Hamon to speak at our conference, but he was already booked that week. We were amazed when Bishop called Dale to say his trip had been cancelled and that he would be free speak at Destiny for an entire weekend. It happened to be the weekend of 10.10.10!

The Lord had already spoken to Dale about Bishop ordaining us as we started into the meetings. Saturday night I asked Dale if he thought that Bishop should ordain us. Dale said that he had asked God to show me, too. Bishop felt like such a father to me. He encouraged me and my ministry. We had a great time with him over those three days. As we were driving to the church Sunday morning, Bishop told us he felt led to ordain us. He felt this was the purpose of his trip to Destiny. That Sunday he ordained us into our apostolic calling and our traveling ministry. It produced a powerful shift in our authority and in our ministry.

Dale and I were praying about the name of our ministry. He had called his "Dale Mast Ministries" for years. But since we were going to travel and minister together, we wanted to make "all things new." Because of the prophetic anointing on his life, we knew there should be an eagle in the name of the ministry. Through my years of ministry I had been known as one who carries the fire of God. We decided to call our ministry "Eagle Fire Ministries." We have traveled together in the USA, Canada, Japan, Korea, Malaysia, and Singapore. Other nations are opening up to us, just as the prophecies I received over all those years spoke of. Even as I am writing this book, opportunities are opening up for me to share my testimony on TV.

Reflection

Writing this book has brought a deeper healing to me. It was an emotional process. The very act of choosing the title stirred up many emotions and brought tears to my eyes. I realized how much loss and pain I walked through during those difficult days. As I finished writing, I became aware of how much I had overcome.

Just thinking about that day sweeping up ashes—a single mom without a car, facing bankruptcy and foreclosure, crying out to the Lord in desperation—it still chokes me up. I was so vulnerable, but I wouldn't give up. If God hadn't been in my life, my situation would have been impossible. I experienced so many miracles and acts of supernatural provision.

I never dreamed God would take me from those ashes to telling my story of restoration around the world with my prince, Dale. What Jesus Christ did for me, He can also do for you. He is no respecter of persons.

It wasn't easy, yet I felt God's presence was the closest to me through the hardest times. He was all I had. When He is all you have, you have all you need.

Faith and obedience are the keys for breaking out of your difficult places and into your future.

The following scriptures help us to understand that the Lord wants to bring healing and restoration to the brokenhearted. May they speak to you as they have spoken to me over the years.

Isaiah 61:1, 3, 7

[1] "The Spirit of the Lord GOD *is* upon Me,
Because the LORD has anointed Me
To preach good tidings to the poor;
He has sent Me to heal the brokenhearted,
To proclaim liberty to the captives,
And the opening of the prison to *those who are* bound.

[3] To console those who mourn in Zion,
To give them beauty for ashes,
The oil of joy for mourning,
The garment of praise for the spirit of heaviness;
That they may be called trees of righteousness,
The planting of the LORD, that He may be glorified."

[7] Instead of your shame *you shall have* double *honor,*
And *instead of* confusion they shall rejoice in their portion.
Therefore in their land they shall possess double;
Everlasting joy shall be theirs.

May the Lord bless you, as He has me.

Much Love,
LuAnne

My "eight red roses."

Be My Wife - BMW

Matthew kissing me goodbye
as they both get ready to hand
me to Dale.

Michael next to us.

Dale and I in the
receiving line.

Cutting the wedding cake.

The father and daughter dance.

Dale and I and all of our children, our wedding party

Our new family photo after the wedding.

On an evening cruise on our honeymoon in
Kona, Hawaii.

Our house at 299 Apple Blossom Drive

My book signing in Seoul, translated into Korean.